Anonymous

Christian Praise

hymns and tunes for public worship

Anonymous

Christian Praise
hymns and tunes for public worship

ISBN/EAN: 9783337089351

Printed in Europe, USA, Canada, Australia, Japan

Cover: Foto ©Lupo / pixelio.de

More available books at **www.hansebooks.com**

CHRISTIAN PRAISE:

HYMNS AND TUNES FOR PUBLIC WORSHIP.

WITH AN INTRODUCTION

BY

THE REV. ROSWELL D. HITCHCOCK, D.D.,

WASHBURN PROFESSOR OF CHURCH HISTORY IN THE UNION
THEOLOGICAL SEMINARY, NEW-YORK.

Let the people praise thee, O God;
Let all the people praise thee.
Psalm 67 : 3, 5.

NEW-YORK:
F. J. HUNTINGTON AND CO.,
459 BROOME STREET.
1870.

Entered, according to Act of Congress, in the year 1870, by
JOHN B. THOMPSON AND
WILLIAM H. PLATT,
In the office of the Librarian of Congress, at Washington.

INTRODUCTION.

The essential elements of public Christian worship are Preaching, Prayer, and Praise. The Ante-Nicene church magnified them all; giving to each of them, not of any set purpose but instinctively, something like its own right proportion and emphasis. Gradually, as the vitality of the church declined, preaching lost its original and legitimate place in the order of service. The old ministry of the word degenerated into a ministry of mere sacraments and ceremonies. Then came the Protestant Reformation, reasserting and reëstablishing the apostolic and primitive dignity of the pulpit.

But extremes always beget extremes. And so it has come about that, in more than one branch of our great Protestant communion, the idea of worship has failed to maintain itself with sufficient vigor alongside of the idea of instruction. In prayer, the deadness of the letter has not always been escaped by discarding liturgical forms. In song especially, there has been too often but a repetition of the sermon.

This extreme is now to be corrected. Indeed, much has already been done towards correcting it. In leading the devotions of the people, many ministers are more studious than they used to be of fitness, fulness, and variety of expression; and, it may be hoped, more careful to go from their closets to the sanctuary charged with the spirit of prayer.

But it is in the service of song that the greatest improvement has been made, at least amongst our American churches. Of the many hymn-books which have recently been published, it might be safe to say, that the poorest are better than the best of those used by our fathers. Didactic, hortatory, and doctrinal hymns have been set aside; fine old hymns revived; and new hymns, inspired by the peculiar Christian life of our own times, added.

The present volume must speak for itself. It is meant to be a choice selection of hymns, and of hymns to be *sung*. The aim has been to have *only*, and yet *all*, those hymns which are actually in use in most of our evangelical churches. Much care has been bestowed upon the music. And here the aim has been to set forth tunes which are at once popular and solid in their character. Years of labor have been expended upon the volume. It is the joint work of two compilers, one of whom is a clergyman of much experience in hymnology, and the other for many years a successful leader of church choirs. I have most cheerfully consented to have my name go upon the title-page, because I have long entertained the ideas which underlie this book, and am happy now to see them so admirably carried out.

ROSWELL D. HITCHCOCK.

Union Theological Seminary,
New-York, Sept. 20, 1870.

PREFACE.

CHRIST is all and in all. In the progress of the race toward perfection in God, this truth is more clearly apprehended than ever before. In this light, old things are passing away. History is rewritten. Theology becomes instinct with life. Devotion becomes more intense. Worship takes on a higher phase. The service of song in the house of the Lord is ennobled. It becomes not only more definitely praise, but also more distinctively "Christian Praise."

From the great mass of material in most hymn-books, the instinct of good pious taste rejects what does not express this developed Christian feeling of the church.

It rejects mere dogmatic statements, as belonging to catechism, creed, confession.

It rejects mere didactic, descriptive, and hortatory rhymes, as belonging to the sermon.

It rejects hymns in praise of deceased saints, angels, or other creatures, the Sunday-school, anniversaries, etc., as foreign to the worship of one God.

It rejects hymns of self-examination in public worship, as belonging rather to the closet.

It rejects poetical compositions which have no lyrical character, as unfitted for musical expression.

Hymns which belong PREVAILINGLY to these classes have been mostly omitted from this book. It is believed, however, that all the really good hymns in the language are here. Some favorite endeared by association may be missed, but a better hymn will probably be found supplying its place.

The fairest flowers into which the Christ-life in the church has blossomed have been culled from every age and every clime. These hymns are therefore catholic as well as Christian. They have not been mutilated and shorn of their power to fit them to any human standard, though many of them have been strengthened by the omission of the weaker verses.

The increasing Christliness of Christianity is increasing the devotional character of public worship. Where this feeling prevails, the hymns used are selected with reference to their emotional character. The arrangement of this book will facilitate such selection. There will be found in each metre a regular gradation in the character of the emotion and the variety of the praise.

The full Topical Index furnishes every facility also for a selection by subjects, and the location of every hymn in a book of this size speedily becomes familiar.

The sentiment of the hymns will generally be well rendered by using either of the tunes opposite.

Music is the language of the emotions, as words are of the intellect. These two languages, in proper combination, must produce a much greater effect than either alone; yet music has been but little studied as a language. Three tunes are therefore given, from which selection may be made at will.

Music is both impressive and expressive.

If the object be to impress the feelings, and prepare for acts of worship, one of the adaptations, or one of the tunes of the higher and more difficult style, may be sung by the trained choir.

If the object be to express the feelings in direct acts of worship, one of the simpler tunes, in which all can join, should be used. This book is specially designed for this end, while fostering also progress in the appreciation of musical language.

There is really no discrepancy between the words and the music of true hymns. Neither need be subordinated to the other. No compromise between them should be attempted, for none is needed. They are naturally adapted to each other. True hymns are compositions of a *lyrical* character, that is, they are *made for music*. All that is necessary, then, is to find the musical language which expresses the sentiment of the hymn, and bring them together. Such music, once

Married to immortal verse,

should never be divorced from it.

The ratification of such union of hymns with tunes by the universal consciousness of the Christian church is one manifestation of her devotional life. Such adaptations sound down through the ages, testifying to the communion of saints. The tunes as well as the hymns in this book represent the devotion of the universal church militant.

The tunes, the hymns, the prayers, the creeds of the church, must alike be the fruit of her own life. The business of the compilers has been to gather a part of this fruit for the convenience of those who partake of it. The enjoyment of communion with the best minds and the highest devotion of the church in this labor of love has been intense. If our labor shall minister to others a tithe of the blessing it has brought to us, we shall rejoice and give thanks.

It remains to acknowledge the kindness of the many clerical and musical friends, to whose suggestions and contributions (which are duly accredited) the book owes much of its value. Special obligation is due to The Rev. Ray Palmer, D.D., without whose valuable hymns no collection can be complete ; to James Flint, Esq., the well-known organist and composer, (who has carefully revised all the music,) for many original contributions; and to U. C. Burnap, Esq., Musical Editor of 'Hymns of the Church,' not only for unrestricted selection from his published tunes, but also for compositions written expressly for this work, and for other valuable assistance in its preparation.

No labor for Christ and His church is insignificant. Great pains were taken with the service of song in the Jewish church, "for so was the commandment of the Lord by His prophets." (2 Chron. xxix. 25–30.) It is an equally important part of Christian worship, both on earth and in heaven. (Eph. v. 19 ; Rev. xiv. 2, 3.) With these views we have labored at this work.

To Him who sang a hymn at the supper in Jerusalem we dedicate it.

To Him be glory forever! Amen.

THE COMPILERS.

1
Psalm 100.

1 BEFORE Jehovah's awful throne,
Ye nations, bow with sacred joy;
Know that the Lord is God alone;
He can create, and He destroy.

2 His sovereign power, without our aid,
Made us of clay, and formed us men;
And when, like wandering sheep, we strayed,
He brought us to His fold again.

3 We are His people, we His care—
Our souls, and all our mortal frame:
What lasting honors shall we rear,
Almighty Maker, to Thy name?

4 We'll crowd Thy gates with thankful songs;
High as the heaven our voices raise;
And earth, with her ten thousand tongues,
Shall fill Thy courts with sounding praise.

5 Wide as the world is Thy command;
Vast as eternity Thy love;
Firm as a rock Thy truth shall stand
When rolling years shall cease to move.

2

1 GREAT One in Three, great Three in One,
Thy wondrous name we sound abroad;
Prostrate we fall before Thy throne,
O holy, holy, holy Lord!

2 Thee, holy Father, we confess;
Thee, holy Saviour, we adore;
And Thee, O Holy Ghost, we bless
And praise and worship evermore.

3 Thou art by heaven and earth adored;
Thy universe is full of Thee,
O holy, holy, holy Lord!
Great Three in One, great One in Three!

3
Psalm 100.

1 ALL people that on earth do dwell,
Sing to the Lord with cheerful voice;
Him serve with mirth, His praise forth tell;
Come ye before Him and rejoice.

2 The Lord, ye know, is God indeed;
Without our aid He did us make;
We are His flock, He doth us feed;
And for His sheep, He doth us take.

3 O enter then His gates with praise;
Approach with joy his courts unto;
Praise, laud, and bless His name always;
For it is seemly so to do.

4 For why, the Lord our God is good;
His mercy is forever sure;
His truth at all times firmly stood,
And shall from age to age endure.

4
Psalm 100.

1 YE nations round the earth rejoice
Before the Lord, your sovereign King;
Serve Him with cheerful heart and voice;
With all your tongues His glory sing.

2 The Lord is God; 'tis He alone
Doth life, and breath, and being give;
We are His work and not our own—
The sheep that on His pastures live.

3 Enter His gates with songs of joy,
With praises to his courts repair,
And make it your divine employ
To pay your thanks and honors there.

4 The Lord is good, the Lord is kind;
Great is His grace, His mercy sure;
And the whole race of man shall find
His truth from age to age endure.

5
Psalm 57.

1 BE Thou exalted, O my God,
Above the heavens where angels dwell;
Thy power on earth be known abroad;
Let land to land Thy wonders tell.

2 My heart is fixed, my song shall raise
Immortal honors to Thy name.
Awake, my tongue, to sound His praise,
My tongue, the glory of my frame.

3 High o'er the earth His mercy reigns,
And reaches to the utmost sky;
His truth to endless years remains,
When lower worlds dissolve and die.

4 Be Thou exalted, O my God,
Above the heavens where angels dwell;
Thy power on earth be known abroad;
Let land to land Thy wonders tell.

6
Psalm 93.

1 Jehovah reigns; He dwells in light,
Girded with majesty and might;
The world, created by His hands,
Still on its firm foundation stands.

2 But ere this spacious world was made,
Or had its first foundation laid,
Thy throne eternal ages stood,
Thyself the ever-living God.

3 Like floods the angry nations rise,
And aim their rage against the skies;
Vain floods that aim their rage so high!
At Thy rebuke the billows die.

4 Forever shall Thy throne endure,
Thy promise stand forever sure;
And everlasting holiness
Becomes the dwelling of Thy grace.

7
Psalm 97.

1 Jehovah reigns; His throne is high,
His robes are light and majesty;
His glory shines with beams so bright
No mortal can sustain the sight.

2 His terrors keep the world in awe;
His justice guards His holy law;
His love reveals a smiling face;
His truth and promise seal the grace.

3 Through all His works His wisdom shines,
And baffles Satan's deep designs;
His power is sovereign to fulfil
The noblest counsels of His will.

4 And will this glorious Lord descend
To be my father and my friend!
Then let my songs with angels join;
Heaven is secure, if God be mine.

8

1 Awake, my tongue! thy tribute bring
To Him who gave thee power to sing;
Praise Him who is all praise above,
The source of wisdom and of love.

2 How vast His knowledge—how profound!
A depth where all our thoughts are drowned!
The stars He numbers, and their names
He gives to all those heavenly flames.

3 Through each bright world above, behold
Ten thousand thousand charms unfold;
Earth, air, and mighty seas combine
To speak His wisdom all divine.

4 But in redemption, O what grace!
Its wonders, O what thought can trace!
Here wisdom shines forever bright—
Praise Him, my soul, with sweet delight.

9

1 Praise, everlasting praise, be paid
To Him who earth's foundation laid;
Praise to the God whose strong decrees
Sway the creation as He please.

2 Praise to the goodness of the Lord,
Who rules His people by His word;
And there, as strong as His decrees,
He sets His kindest promises.

3 O for a strong, a lasting faith,
To credit what th' Almighty saith;
T' embrace the message of His Son,
And call the joys of heaven our own.

4 Then, should the earth's old pillars shake,
And all the wheels of nature break,
Our steady souls would fear no more
Than solid rocks when billows roar.

10
Psalm 93.

1 With glory clad, with strength arrayed,
The Lord that o'er all nature reigns,
The world's foundation strongly laid,
And the vast fabric still sustains.

2 How surely stablished is Thy throne,
Which shall no change nor period see;
For Thou, O Lord, and Thou alone,
Art God from all eternity.

3 The floods, O Lord, lift up their voice,
And toss their troubled waves on high;
But God above can still their noise,
And make the angry sea comply.

4 Thy promise, Lord, is ever sure,
And they that in Thy house would dwell,
That happy station to secure,
Must still in holiness excel.

11
Psalm 97.

1 He reigns! the Lord, the Saviour reigns!
Praise Him in evangelic strains:
Let the whole earth in songs rejoice,
And distant islands join their voice.

2 Deep are His counsels, and unknown;
But grace and truth support His throne;
Though gloomy clouds His ways surround,
Justice is their eternal ground.

3 In robes of judgment, lo, He comes,
Shakes the wide earth, and cleaves the tombs!
Before Him burns devouring fire;
The mountains melt, the seas retire!

4 His enemies, with sore dismay,
Fly from the sight, and shun the day:
Then lift your heads, ye saints, on high,
And sing, for your redemption's nigh!

12
Psalm 97.

1 The Lord is King! lift up thy voice,
O earth, and all ye heavens, rejoice!
From world to world the joy shall ring:
The Lord omnipotent is King!

2 The Lord is King! who then shall dare
Resist His will, distrust His care!
Holy and true are all His ways;
Let every creature speak His praise.

3 The Lord is King! exalt your strains,
Ye saints; your God, your Father, reigns;
One Lord, one empire, all secures;
He reigns—and life and death are yours.

4 O when His wisdom can mistake,
His might decay, His love forsake,
Then may His children cease to sing
The Lord omnipotent is King!

13

1 Stand up, my soul, shake off thy fears,
And gird the gospel armor on;
March to the gates of endless joy,
Where Jesus, thy great Captain's gone.

2 Hell and thy sins resist thy course,
But hell and sin are vanquished foes;
Thy Jesus nailed them to the cross,
And sung the triumph when He rose.

3 Then let my soul march boldly on,
Press forward to the heavenly gate;
There peace and joy eternal reign,
And glittering robes for conquerors wait.

4 There shall I wear a starry crown,
And triumph in Almighty grace,
While all the armies of the skies
Join in my glorious Leader's praise.

14
Psalm 136.

1 Give to our God immortal praise;
Mercy and truth are all His ways;
Wonders of grace to God belong:
Repeat His mercies in your song.

2 Give to the Lord of lords renown,
The King of kings with glory crown;
His mercies ever shall endure,
When lords and kings are known no more.

3 He built the earth, He spread the sky,
And fixed the starry lights on high;
Wonders of grace to God belong:
Repeat His mercies in your song.

4 He fills the sun with morning-light,
He bids the moon direct the night:
His mercies ever shall endure,
When suns and moons shall shine no more.

5 He sent His Son, with power to save
From guilt, and darkness, and the grave;
Wonders of grace to God belong:
Repeat His mercies in your song.

15
Psalm 138.

1 With all my powers of heart and tongue,
I'll praise my Maker in my song;
Angels shall hear the notes I raise,
Approve the song, and join the praise.

2 To God I cried when troubles rose;
He heard me, and subdued my foes;
He did my rising fears control,
And strength diffused through all my soul.

3 I'll sing Thy truth and mercy, Lord,
I'll sing the wonders of Thy word;
Not all Thy works and names below
So much Thy power and glory show.

16

1 Now to the Lord a noble song!
   Awake, my soul! awake, my tongue!
   Hosanna to the eternal Name,
   And all His boundless love proclaim.

2 See where it shines in Jesus' face—
   The brightest image of His grace!
   God, in the person of His Son,
   Has all His mightiest works outdone.

3 Grace!—'tis a sweet, a charming theme;
   My thoughts rejoice at Jesus' name:
   Ye angels! dwell upon the sound;
   Ye heavens! reflect it to the ground.

4 O may I reach that happy place
   Where He unveils His lovely face;
   Where all His beauties you behold,
   And sing His name to harps of gold!

17   Psalm 95.

1 O come, loud anthems let us sing,
   Loud thanks to our Almighty King!
   For we our voices high should raise
   When our salvation's Rock we praise.

2 Into His presence let us haste
   To thank Him for His favors past;
   To Him address in joyful songs
   The praise that to His Name belongs.

3 O let us to His courts repair,
   And bow with adoration there;
   With humble souls adore His grace,
   And kneel before our Maker's face.

18   Psalm 148.

1 Loud hallelujahs to the Lord,
   From distant worlds where creatures dwell!
   Let heaven begin the solemn word,
   And sound it dreadful down to hell.

2 Wide as His vast dominion lies,
   Make the Creator's name be known;
   Loud as His thunder shout His praise,
   And sound it lofty as His throne.

3 Jehovah! 'tis a glorious word!
   O may it dwell on every tongue;
   But saints who best have known the Lord,
   Are bound to raise the noblest song.

19

1 Come, O my soul, in sacred lays,
   Attempt thy great Creator's praise;
   But O what tongue can speak His fame!
   What mortal verse can reach the theme!

2 Enthroned amidst the radiant spheres,
   He glory, like a garment, wears;
   To form a robe of light divine
   Ten thousand suns around Him shine.

3 In all our Maker's grand designs,
   Omnipotence with wisdom shines;
   His works through all His wondrous frame
   Bear the great impress of His name.

4 Raised on devotion's lofty wing,
   Do thou, my soul, His glories sing;
   And let His praise employ thy tongue,
   Till listening worlds repeat the song.

20   Psalm 107.

1 Give thanks to God, He reigns above;
   Kind are His thoughts, His name is love;
   His mercy ages past have known,
   And ages long to come shall own.

2 Let the redeemed of the Lord
   The wonders of His grace record;
   Israel, the nation whom He chose,
   And rescued from their mighty foes.

3 He feeds and clothes us all the way,
   He guides our footsteps, lest we stray;
   He guards us with a powerful hand,
   And brings us to the heavenly land.

4 O let us, then, with joy record
   The truth and goodness of the Lord;
   How great His works—how kind His ways!
   Let every tongue pronounce His praise.

21   Psalm 117.

1 From all that dwell below the skies,
   Let the Creator's praise arise;
   Let the Redeemer's name be sung
   Through every land, by every tongue.

2 Eternal are Thy mercies, Lord;
   Eternal truth attends Thy word;
   Thy praise shall sound from shore to shore,
   Till suns shall rise and set no more.

22
Psalm 72.

1 Jesus shall reign where'er the sun
Does His successive journeys run;
His kingdom stretch from shore to shore,
Till moons shall wax and wane no more.

2 For Him shall endless prayer be made,
And praises throng to crown His head;
His name like sweet perfume shall rise
With every morning sacrifice.

3 People and realms of every tongue
Dwell on His love with sweetest song;
And infant voices shall proclaim
Their early blessings on His Name.

4 Blessings abound where'er He reigns;
The prisoner leaps to lose his chains,
The weary find eternal rest,
And all the sons of want are blest.

5 Let every creature rise and bring
Peculiar honors to our King;
Angels descend with songs again,
And earth repeat the loud Amen!

23

1 Ride on! ride on in majesty!
Hark! all the tribes Hosanna cry:
O Saviour meek, pursue Thy road
With palms and scattered garments strowed.

2 Ride on! ride on in majesty!
In lowly pomp, ride on to die:
O Christ, Thy triumphs now begin
O'er captive death and conquered sin.

3 Ride on! ride on in majesty!
The angel armies of the sky
Look down with sad and wondering eyes
To see the approaching sacrifice.

4 Ride on! ride on in majesty!
The last and fiercest strife is nigh:
The Father on his sapphire Throne
Awaits His own anointed Son.

5 Ride on! ride on in majesty!
In lowly pomp, ride on to die;
Bow Thy meek head to mortal pain,
Then take, O God, Thy power, and reign.

24

1 Descend from heaven, immortal Dove!
Stoop down, and take us on Thy wings,
And mount, and bear us far above
The reach of these inferior things—

2 Beyond, beyond this lower sky,
Up where eternal ages roll,
Where solid pleasures never die,
And fruits immortal feast the soul.

3 O for a sight, a blissful sight
Of our almighty Father's throne!
There sits the Saviour, crowned with light,
Clothed in a body like our own.

4 Adoring saints around Him stand,
And thrones and powers before Him fall;
The God shines gracious through the Man,
And sheds sweet glories on them all.

5 O what amazing joys they feel,
While to their golden harps they sing,
And sit on every heavenly hill,
And spread the triumph of their King!

25

1 Great God! let all our tuneful powers
Awake, and sing Thy mighty Name:
Thy hand revolves our circling hours—
Thy hand from which our being came.

2 Seasons and moons still rolling round,
In beauteous order speak Thy praise;
And years, with smiling mercy crowned,
To Thee successive honors raise.

3 To Thee we raise the annual song,
To Thee the grateful tribute give;
Our God doth still our years prolong,
And, 'midst unnumbered deaths, we live.

4 Our life, our health, our friends, we owe
All to Thy vast, unbounded love;
Ten thousand precious gifts below,
And hope of nobler joys above.

5 Thus will we sing, till nature cease,
Till sense and language are no more,
And, after death, Thy boundless grace,
Through everlasting years adore.

26
Psalm 19.

1 The heavens declare Thy glory, Lord,
In every star Thy wisdom shines;
But when our eyes behold Thy word,
We read Thy name in fairer lines.

2 The rolling sun, the changing light,
And nights and days Thy power confess;
But the blest volume Thou hast writ,
Reveals Thy justice and Thy grace.

3 Sun, moon, and stars convey Thy praise
Round the whole earth, and never stand;
So when Thy truth began its race,
It touched and glanced on every land.

4 Nor shall Thy spreading gospel rest,
Till through the world Thy truth has run;
Till Christ has all the nations blest,
That see the light or feel the sun.

5 Thy noblest wonders here we view,
In souls renewed, and sins forgiven:
Lord! cleanse my sins, my soul renew,
And make Thy word my guide to heaven.

27
Psalm 145.

1 My God, my King, Thy various praise
Shall fill the remnant of my days;
Thy grace employ my humble tongue,
Till death and glory raise the song.

2 The wings of every hour shall bear
Some thankful tribute to Thine ear;
And every setting sun shall see
New works of duty done for Thee.

3 Let distant times and nations raise
The long succession of Thy praise;
And unborn ages make my song
The joy and triumph of their tongue.

4 But who can speak Thy wondrous deeds!
Thy greatness all our thoughts exceeds;
Vast and unsearchable Thy ways!
Vast and immortal be Thy praise!

28
Psalm 19.

1 The spacious firmament on high,
With all the blue ethereal sky,
And spangled heavens, a shining frame,
Their great Original proclaim.

2 The unwearied sun, from day to day,
Does his Creator's power display,
And publishes to every land
The work of an Almighty hand.

3 Soon as the evening shades prevail,
The moon takes up the wondrous tale,
And nightly to the listening earth,
Repeats the story of her birth;

4 While all the stars that round her burn,
And all the planets in their turn,
Confirm the tidings as they roll,
And spread the truth from pole to pole.

5 What though in solemn silence all
Move round this dark terrestrial ball;
What though no real voice nor sound
Amid their radiant orbs be found;

6 In reason's ear they all rejoice,
And utter forth a glorious voice,
Forever singing as they shine—
"The hand that made us is divine."

29

1 Awake, my soul, and with the sun
Thy daily stage of duty run;
Shake off dull sloth, and joyful rise
To pay thy morning sacrifice.

2 Wake and lift up thyself, my heart,
And with the angels bear thy part,
Who, all night long, unwearied sing
High praise to the Eternal King.

3 All praise to Thee who safe hast kept,
And hast refreshed me while I slept!
Grant, Lord, when I from death shall wake,
I may of endless life partake!

4 Lord, I my vows to Thee renew;
Disperse my sins as morning dew;
Guard my first springs of thought and will,
And with Thyself my spirit fill.

5 Praise God from whom all blessings flow!
Praise Him, all creatures here below!
Praise Him above, ye heavenly host!
Praise Father, Son, and Holy Ghost!

30   Psalm 45.

1 Now be my heart inspired to sing
The glories of my Saviour-King—
Jesus, the Lord; how heavenly fair
His form! how bright His beauties are!

2 O'er all the sons of human race
He shines with a superior grace;
Love from His lips divinely flows,
And blessings all His state compose.

3 Thy throne, O God, forever stands;
Grace is the sceptre in Thy hands;
Thy laws and works are just and right;
Justice and grace are Thy delight.

4 God! Thine own God has richly shed
His oil of gladness on Thy head;
And with His sacred Spirit blessed
His first-born Son above the rest.

31   Psalm 84.

1 Great God, attend while Zion sings
The joy that from Thy presence springs;
To spend one day with Thee on earth,
Exceeds a thousand days of mirth.

2 Might I enjoy the meanest place
Within Thy house, O God of grace,
Not tents of ease, nor thrones of power,
Should tempt my feet to leave Thy door.

3 God is our Sun, He makes our day;
God is our Shield, He guards our way
From all the assaults of hell and sin,
From foes without and foes within.

4 All needful grace will God bestow,
And crown that grace with glory too;
He gives us all things, and withholds
No real good from upright souls.

32   Psalm 103.

1 Bless, O my soul, the living God,
Call home Thy thoughts that rove abroad;
Let all the powers within me join
In work and worship so divine.

2 Bless, O my soul, the God of grace;
His favors claim thy highest praise;
Why should the wonders He hath wrought
Be lost in silence, and forgot!

3 Let the whole earth His power confess,
Let the whole earth adore His grace;
The Gentile with the Jew shall join,
In work and worship so divine.

33   Psalm 106.

1 O render thanks to God above,
The fountain of eternal love,
Whose mercy firm through ages past
Hath stood, and shall forever last.

2 Who can His mighty deeds express,
Not only vast but numberless!
What mortal eloquence can raise
His tribute of immortal praise!

3 Extend to me that favor, Lord,
Thou to Thy chosen dost afford;
When Thou return'st to set them free,
Let Thy salvation visit me.

4 O may I worthy prove to see
Thy saints in full prosperity,
That I the joyful choir may join,
And count Thy people's triumph mine.

34   Psalm 72.

1 Great God, whose universal sway
The known and unknown worlds obey,
Now give the kingdom to Thy Son,
Extend His power, exalt His throne.

2 Thy sceptre well becomes His hands;
All heaven submits to His commands;
His justice shall avenge the poor,
And pride and rage prevail no more.

3 As rain on meadows newly mown,
So shall He send His influence down;
His grace on fainting souls distils,
Like heavenly dew on thirsty hills.

4 The heathen lands that lie beneath
The shades of overspreading death,
Revive at His first dawning light,
And deserts blossom at the sight.

5 The saints shall flourish in His days,
Dressed in the robes of joy and praise·
Peace, like a river from His throne,
Shall flow to nations yet unknown.

35

1 When marshalled on the nightly plain,
The glittering host be- | stud the | sky,
One star alone of all the train
Can fix the | sinner's | wandering | eye.
Hark! hark! to God the chorus breaks
From every host, from | every | gem;
But one alone the Saviour speaks,
It is the | Star—the | Star of | Bethlehem.

2 Once on the raging seas I rode,
The storm was loud, the | night was | dark,
The ocean yawned, and rudely blowed
The wind that | tossed my | foundering | bark.
Deep horror then my vitals froze;
Death-struck, I ceased the | tide to | stem,
When suddenly a star arose,
It was the | Star—the | Star of | Bethlehem.

3 It was my guide, my light, my all;
It bade my dark fore- | bodings | cease;
And through the storm, and danger's thrall,
It led me | to the | port of | peace.
Now safely moored, my perils o'er,
I'll sing | first—in night's | diadem,
Forever and for evermore,
The | Star—the | Star of | Bethlehem!

36
Psalm 17.

1 What sinners value I resign;
Lord, 'tis enough that | Thou art | mine;
I shall behold Thy blissful face,
And stand com- | plete in | righteous- | ness.

2 This life's a dream, an empty show,
But the bright world to | which I | go
Hath joys substantial and sincere;
When shall I | wake and | find me | there!

3 O glorious hour! O blest abode!
I shall be near and | like my | God,
And flesh and sin no more control
The sacred | pleasures | of the | soul.

4 My flesh shall slumber in the ground
Till the last trumpet's | joyful | sound;
Then burst the chains with sweet surprise,
And in my | Saviour's | image | rise.

37

1 O Saviour, who for man hast trod
The winepress of the | wrath of | God,
Ascend and claim again on high
Thy glory | left for | us to | die.

2 A radiant cloud is now Thy seat,
And earth lies stretched be- | neath Thy | feet; [sing,
Ten thousand thousands round Thee
And share the | triumph | of their | King.

3 The angel host enraptured waits;
"Lift up your heads, e- | ternal | gates!"
O God-and-Man! the Father's throne
Is now, for | ever- | more, Thine | own.

4 Our great High-Priest and Shepherd, Thou
Within the veil art | entered | now,
To offer there Thy precious blood,
Once poured on | earth a | cleansing | flood.

5 And thence the church, Thy chosen bride,
With countless gifts of | grace supplied,
Through all her members draws from Thee
Her hidden | life of | sancti- | ty.

6 O Christ, our Lord, of Thy dear care
Thy lowly members | heavenward | bear;
Be ours with Thee to suffer pain,
With Thee for | ever- | more to | reign.

38

1 When Jordan hushed his waters still,
And silence slept on | Zion's | hill;
When Bethlehem's shepherds through the night
Watched o'er their | flocks by | starry | light;

2 On wheels of light, on wings of flame,
The glorious hosts of | Zion | came;
High heaven with songs of triumph rung,
While thus they | struck their | harps, and | sung:

3 "O Zion, lift thy raptured eye!
The long-expected | hour is | nigh;
Renewed, creation smiles again,
The Prince of | Salem | comes to | reign.

4 "He comes to cheer the trembling heart,
Bid Satan and his | host de- | part;
Again the Daystar gilds the gloom,
Again the | bowers of | Eden | bloom."

39

1 O HAPPY day, that stays my choice
On Thee, my Saviour and my God!
Well may this glowing heart rejoice,
And tell its raptures all abroad.

2 O happy bond, that seals my vows
To Him who merits all my love!
Let cheerful anthems fill His house,
While to that sacred shrine I move.

3 'Tis done, the great transaction's done!
I am my Lord's, and He is mine;
He drew me, and I followed on,
Glad to obey the voice divine.

4 Now rest, my long divided heart,
Fixed on this blissful centre, rest;
With ashes who would grudge to part,
When called on angels' bread to feast!

5 High heaven that heard the solemn vow,
That vow renewed shall daily hear,
Till in life's latest hour I bow,
And bless in death a bond so dear.

40

1 WHEN sins and fears prevailing rise,
And fainting hope almost expires,
Jesus, to Thee I lift mine eyes;
To Thee I breathe my soul's desires.

2 If my immortal Saviour lives,
Then my immortal life is sure;
His word a firm foundation gives;
Here may I build and rest secure.

3 Here let my faith unshaken dwell;
Immovable the promise stands;
Not all the powers of earth or hell
Can e'er dissolve the sacred bands.

4 Here, O my soul, Thy trust repose;
If Jesus is forever mine,
Not death itself, that last of foes,
Shall break a union so divine.

41

1 Now to the Lord, who makes us know
The wonders of His dying love,
Be humble honors paid below,
And strains of nobler praise above.

2 'Twas He that cleansed our foulest sins,
And washed us in His richest blood;
'Tis He that makes us priests and kings,
And brings us rebels near to God.

3 To Jesus, our atoning priest,
To Jesus, our superior king,
Be everlasting power confessed,
And every tongue His glory sing.

42

1 Now I resolve with all my heart,
With all my powers, to serve the Lord;
Nor from His ways will I depart,
Whose service is a rich reward.

2 O be this service all my joy!
Around let my example shine,
Till others love the blest employ,
And join in labors so divine.

3 Be this the purpose of my soul,
My solemn, my determined choice,
To yield to His supreme control,
And in His kind commands rejoice.

4 O may I never faint nor tire,
Nor wandering, leave His sacred ways;
Great God, accept my soul's desire,
And give me strength to live Thy praise.

43

1 THINE earthly Sabbaths, Lord, we love,
But there's a nobler rest above;
To that our laboring souls aspire
With ardent pangs of strong desire.

2 No more fatigue, no more distress;
Nor sin, nor hell, shall reach the place;
No groans to mingle with the songs
Which warble from immortal tongues;

3 No rude alarms of raging foes,
No cares to break the long repose;
No midnight shade, no clouded sun,
But sacred, high, eternal noon.

4 O long-expected day, begin,
Dawn on these realms of woe and sin!
Fain would we leave this weary road,
And sleep in death to rest with God.

44
Psalm 92.

1 Sweet is the work, my God, my King,
  To praise Thy name, give thanks and sing;
  To show Thy love by morning light,
  And talk of all Thy truth at night.

2 My heart shall triumph in my Lord,
  And bless His works, and bless His word:
  Thy works of grace, how bright they shine!
  How deep Thy counsels, how divine!

3 Lord, I shall share a glorious part
  When grace hath well refined my heart;
  And fresh supplies of joy are shed,
  Like holy oil, to cheer my head.

4 Then shall I see, and hear, and know,
  All I desired or wished below;
  And every power find sweet employ
  In that eternal world of joy.

45

1 Jesus, Thy Blood and Righteousness
  My beauty are, my glorious dress;
  'Midst flaming worlds, in these arrayed,
  With joy shall I lift up my head.

2 When from the dust of death I rise,
  To claim my mansion in the skies,
  E'en then, shall this be all my plea:
  Jesus hath lived, hath died for me.

3 This spotless robe the same appears,
  When ruined nature sinks in years;
  No age can change its glorious hue,
  The robe of Christ is ever new.

4 O let the dead now hear Thy voice!
  Bid, Lord, Thy mourning ones rejoice;
  Their beauty this, their glorious dress,
  Jesus, the Lord our Righteousness.

46
Psalm 84.

1 How pleasant, how divinely fair,
  O Lord of hosts, Thy dwellings are!
  With long desire my spirit faints
  To meet the assemblies of Thy saints.

2 Blest are the saints who sit on high
  Around Thy throne of majesty;
  Thy brightest glories shine above,
  And all their work is praise and love.

3 Blest are the souls that find a place
  Within the temple of Thy grace;
  There they behold Thy gentler rays,
  And seek Thy face and learn Thy praise.

4 Cheerful they walk with growing strength,
  Till all shall meet in heaven at length;
  Till all before Thy face appear,
  And join in nobler worship there.

47

1 Come, dearest Lord, descend and dwell,
  By faith and love in every breast;
  Then shall we know, and taste, and feel
  The joys that cannot be expressed.

2 Come, fill our hearts with inward strength,
  Make our enlarged souls possess
  And learn the height, and breadth, and length
  Of Thine unmeasurable grace.

3 Now to the God whose power can do
  More than our thoughts and wishes know,
  Be everlasting honors done,
  By all the church, through Christ the Son.

48

1 Another six days' work is done;
  Another Sabbath is begun.
  Return, my soul, enjoy the rest;
  Improve the day thy God hath blest.

2 O that our thoughts and thanks may rise
  As grateful incense to the skies;
  And draw from heaven that sweet repose
  Which none but he that feels it knows.

3 This heavenly calm within the breast
  Is the dear pledge of glorious rest
  Which for the church of God remains,
  The end of cares, the end of pains.

4 In holy duties let the day .
  In holy pleasures pass away.
  How sweet a Sabbath thus to spend,
  In hope of one that ne'er shall end!

49

1 GLORY to Thee, my God, this night,
  For all the blessings of the light;
  Keep me, O keep me, King of kings,
  Beneath Thine own Almighty wings.

2 Forgive me, Lord, for Thy dear Son,
  The ill that I this day have done;
  That with the world, myself, and Thee,
  I, ere I sleep, at peace may be.

3 Teach me to live, that I may dread
  The grave as little as my bed;
  Teach me to die, that so I may
  Rise glorious at the awful day.

4 O may my soul on Thee repose;
  And may sweet sleep mine eyelids close,
  That shall my frame more vig'rous make,
  To serve my God when I awake.

5 Praise God, from whom all blessings flow;
  Praise Him, all creatures here below;
  Praise Him above, ye heavenly host;
  Praise Father, Son, and Holy Ghost!

50

1 JESUS, and shall it ever be,
  A mortal man ashamed of Thee!
  Ashamed of Thee whom angels praise!
  Whose glories shine through endless days!

2 Ashamed of Jesus!—sooner far
  Let evening blush to own a star;
  He sheds the beams of light divine
  O'er this benighted soul of mine.

3 Ashamed of Jesus!—that dear Friend
  On whom my hopes of heaven depend!
  No! when I blush, be this my shame,
  That I no more revere His name.

4 Ashamed of Jesus!—yes, I may,
  When I've no guilt to wash away,
  No tear to wipe, no good to crave,
  No fear to quell, no soul to save.

5 Till then, nor is my boasting vain,
  Till then, I boast a Saviour slain!
  And O may this my glory be,
  That Christ is not ashamed of me!

51

1 No more, my God, I boast no more
  Of all the duties I have done;
  I quit the hopes I held before,
  To trust the merits of Thy Son.

2 Now, for the love I bear His name,
  What was my gain I count my loss;
  My former pride I call my shame,
  And nail my glory to His cross.

3 Yes, and I must and will esteem
  All things but loss for Jesus' sake:
  O may my soul be found in Him,
  And of His righteousness partake!

4 The best obedience of my hands
  Dares not appear before Thy throne;
  But faith can answer Thy demands,
  By pleading what my Lord has done.

52

1 GOD, in the gospel of His Son,
  Makes His eternal counsels known:
  Here love in all its glory shines,
  And truth is drawn in fairest lines.

2 Here sinners of a humble frame
  May taste His grace, and learn His Name;
  May read, in characters of blood,
  The wisdom, power, and grace of God.

3 Here faith reveals to mortal eyes
  A brighter world beyond the skies;
  Here shines the light which guides our way
  From earth to realms of endless day.

4 O grant us grace, Almighty Lord,
  To read and mark Thy holy word,
  Its truths with meekness to receive,
  And by its holy precepts live.

53

1 THUS far the Lord hath led me on,
  Thus far His power prolongs my days;
  And every evening shall make known
  Some fresh memorial of His grace.

2 I lay my body down to sleep;
  Peace is the pillow for my head,
  While well-appointed angels keep
  Their watchful stations round my bed.

54

1 O WONDROUS type, O vision fair,
Of glory that the church shall share,
Which Christ upon the mountain shows,
Where brighter than the sun He glows!

2 With shining face and bright array,
Christ deigns to manifest to-day
What glory shall be theirs above
Who joy in God with perfect love.

3 And faithful hearts are raised on high
By this great vision's mystery;
For which in joyful strains we raise
The voice of prayer, the hymn of praise.

4 O Father, with the eternal Son,
And Holy Spirit, ever One,
Vouchsafe to bring us by Thy grace
To see Thy glory face to face.

55

1 I KNOW that my Redeemer lives;
What comfort this sweet sentence gives!
He lives, He lives, who once was dead;
He lives, my ever-living Head!

2 He lives to bless me with His love;
He lives to plead for me above;
He lives to calm my troubled heart;
He lives all blessings to impart.

3 He lives, my kind, wise, heavenly Friend;
He lives, and loves me to the end.
He lives, and while He lives I'll sing;
He lives, my Prophet, Priest, and King.

4 He lives, all glory to His name;
He lives, my Jesus, still the same;
O the sweet joy this sentence gives,
I know that my Redeemer lives.

56

1 JESUS, Thy boundless love to me
No thought can reach, no tongue declare;
O knit my thankful heart to Thee,
And reign without a rival there.

2 Thy love, how cheering is its ray!
All pain before its presence flies;
Care, anguish, sorrow melt away,
Where'er its healing beams arise.

3 O let Thy love my soul inflame,
And to Thy service sweetly bind;
Transfuse it through my inmost frame
And mould me wholly to Thy mind.

4 Thy love in suffering be my peace;
Thy love in weakness make me strong;
And when the storms of life shall cease,
Thy love shall be my heaven and song.

57

1 JESUS, Thou joy of loving hearts!
Thou fount of life! Thou light of men!
From the best bliss that earth imparts
We turn, unfilled, to Thee again.

2 We taste Thee, O Thou living bread,
And long to feast upon Thee still;
We drink of Thee, the fountain-head,
And thirst our souls from Thee to fill.

3 Our restless spirits yearn for Thee
Where'er our changeful lot is cast;
Glad when Thy gracious smile we see,
Blest when our faith can hold Thee fast.

4 O Jesus, ever with us stay,
Make all our moments calm and bright,
Chase the dark night of sin away,
Shed o'er the world Thy holy light.

58

1 HE lives! the great Redeemer lives!
What joy the blest assurance gives!
And now before His Father, God,
Pleads the full merit of His blood.

2 Repeated crimes awake our fears,
And justice armed with frowns appears;
But in the Saviour's lovely face
Sweet mercy smiles, and all is peace.

3 In every dark, distressful hour,
When sin and Satan join their power,
Let this dear hope repel the dart,
That Jesus bears us on His heart.

4 Great Advocate! Almighty Friend!
On Him our humble hopes depend;
Our cause can never, never fail,
For Jesus pleads, and must prevail.

59

1 GREAT God, to Thee my evening song
  With humble gratitude I raise;
  O let Thy mercy tune my tongue,
  And fill my heart with lively praise.

2 My days unclouded as they pass,
  And every gently rolling hour,
  Are monuments of wondrous grace,
  And witness to Thy love and power.

3 And yet this thoughtless, wretched heart,
  Too oft regardless of Thy love,
  Ungrateful, can from Thee depart,
  And, fond of trifles, vainly rove.

4 Seal my forgiveness in the blood
  Of Jesus; His dear name alone
  I plead for pardon, gracious God,
  And kind acceptance at Thy throne.

5 Let this blest hope mine eyelids close;
  With sleep refresh my feeble frame;
  Safe in Thy care may I repose,
  And wake with praises to Thy Name!

60

1. O SWEETLY breathe the lyres above,
  When angels touch the quivering string,
  And wake, to chant Immanuel's love,
  Such strains as angel lips can sing!

2 And sweet on earth the choral swell,
  From mortal tongues, of gladsome lays,
  When pardoned souls their raptures tell,
  And, grateful, hymn Immanuel's praise.

3 Jesus, Thy name our souls adore;
  We own the bond that makes us Thine,
  And earthly joys, that charmed before,
  For Thy dear sake we now resign.

4 Our hearts, by dying love subdued,
  Accept Thine offered grace to-day;
  Beneath the cross, with blood bedewed,
  We bow and give ourselves away.

5 In Thee we trust, on Thee rely;
  Though we are feeble, Thou art strong;
  O keep us till our spirits fly
  To join the bright immortal throng!

61

1 ETERNAL Source of every joy,
  Well may Thy praise our lips employ,
  While in Thy temple we appear
  To hail Thee, Sovereign of the year.

2 Wide as the wheels of nature roll,
  Thy hand supports and guides the whole;
  The sun is taught by Thee to rise,
  And darkness when to veil the skies.

3 The flowery spring, at Thy command,
  Perfumes the air and paints the land;
  The summer rays with vigor shine
  To raise the corn and cheer the vine.

4 Thy hand, in autumn, richly pours
  Through all our coasts redundant stores;
  And winters, softened by Thy care,
  No more the face of horror wear.

5 Seasons, and months, and weeks, and days
  Demand successive songs of praise;
  And be the grateful homage paid,
  With morning light and evening shade.

6 Here in Thy house let incense rise,
  And circling Sabbaths bless our eyes;
  Till to those lofty heights we soar
  Where days and years revolve no more.

62

1 GREAT God, we sing that mighty hand
  By which supported still we stand:
  The opening year Thy mercy shows;
  Let mercy crown it till it close.

2 By day, by night, at home, abroad,
  Still we are guarded by our God;
  By His incessant bounty fed,
  By his unerring counsel led.

3 With grateful hearts the past we own;
  The future, all to us unknown,
  We to Thy guardian care commit,
  And peaceful leave before Thy feet.

4 In scenes exalted or deprest,
  Be Thou our joy, and Thou our rest!
  Thy goodness all our hopes shall raise,
  Adored through all our changing days.

63

1 Come, gracious Spirit, heavenly Dove,
With light and comfort from above;
Be Thou our guardian, Thou our guide,
O'er every thought and step preside.

2 To us the light of truth display,
And makes us know and choose Thy way;
Plant holy fear in every heart,
That we from God may ne'er depart.

3 Lead us to holiness, the road
That we must take to dwell with God;
Lead us to Christ, the living way,
Nor let us from his precepts stray.

4 Lead us to God, our final rest,
To be with Him forever blessed;
Lead us to heaven, its bliss to share,
And drink our fill of pleasure there.

64

1 Sweet peace of conscience, heavenly guest!
Come, fix thy mansion in my breast;
Dispel my doubts, my fears control,
And heal the anguish of my soul.

2 Come, smiling hope! and joy sincere!
Come, make your constant dwelling here;
Still let your presence cheer my heart,
Nor sin compel you to depart.

3 Thou God of hope and peace divine!
O make these sacred pleasures mine;
Forgive my sins, my fears remove,
And send the tokens of Thy love.

4 Then should mine eyes, without a tear,
See death with all its terrors near;
My heart should then in death rejoice,
And raptures tune my faltering voice.

65   Psalm 63.

1 Great God, indulge my humble claim;
Thou art my hope, my joy, my rest;
The glories that compose Thy name
Stand all engaged to make me blest.

2 Thou great and good, Thou just and wise,
Thou art my Father and my God;
And I am Thine, by sacred ties,
Thy son, Thy servant, bought with blood.

3 With heart, and eyes, and lifted hands,
For Thee I long, to Thee I look,
As travellers in thirsty lands,
Pant for the cooling water brook.

4 With early feet I love to appear
Among Thy saints, and seek Thy face;
Oft have I seen Thy glory there,
And felt the power of sovereign grace.

5 I'll lift my hands, I'll raise my voice,
While I have breath to pray or praise;
This work shall make my heart rejoice,
And cheer the remnant of my days.

66

1 Thou only Sovereign of my heart,
My Refuge, my Almighty Friend,
And can my soul from Thee depart,
On whom alone my hopes depend!

2 Eternal life Thy words impart;
On these my fainting spirit lives;
Here sweeter comforts cheer my heart
Than all the round of nature gives.

3 Thy Name my inmost powers adore;
Thou art my life, my joy, my care;
Depart from Thee! 'tis death, 'tis more—
'Tis endless ruin, deep despair!

4 Low at Thy feet my soul would lie;
Here safety dwells, and peace divine;
Still let me live beneath Thine eye,
For life, eternal life, is Thine.

67

1 My God, how endless is Thy love!
Thy gifts are every evening new;
And morning mercies from above
Gently distil like early dew.

2 Thou spread'st the curtains of the night,
Great Guardian of my sleeping hours;
Thy sovereign word restores the light,
And quickens all my drowsy powers.

3 I yield my powers to Thy command;
To Thee I consecrate my days;
Perpetual blessings from Thy hand
Demand perpetual songs of praise.

68

1 Lord! Thou hast searched and seen me through;
Thine eye commands, with piercing view,
My rising and my resting hours,
My heart and flesh, with all their powers.

2 My thoughts, before they are my own,
Are to my God distinctly known;
He knows the words I mean to speak,
Ere from my opening lips they break.

3 Within Thy circling power I stand,
On every side I find Thy hand;
Awake, asleep, at home, abroad,
I am surrounded still with God.

4 O may these thoughts possess my breast,
Where'er I rove, where'er I rest;
Nor let my weaker passions dare
Consent to sin, for God is there.

69

1 Through every age, eternal God,
Thou art our rest, our safe abode;
High was Thy throne ere heaven was made,
Or earth Thy humble footstool laid.

2 Long hadst Thou reigned ere time began,
Or dust was fashioned to a man;
And long Thy kingdom shall endure,
When earth and time shall be no more.

3 But man, weak man, is born to die,
Made up of guilt and vanity;
Thy dreadful sentence, Lord, was just,
"Return, ye sinners! to your dust."

4 Death like an overflowing stream
Sweeps us away; our life's a dream,
An empty tale, a morning flower
Cut down and withered in an hour.

70 *Psalm 46.*

1 God is the refuge of His saints
When storms of sharp distress invade;
Ere we can offer our complaints,
Behold Him present with His aid.

2 Let mountains from their seats be hurled
Down to the deep, and buried there;
Convulsions shake the solid world,
Our faith shall never yield to fear.

3 There is a stream whose gentle flow
Supplies the city of our God;
Life, love, and joy, still gliding through,
And watering our divine abode.

4 That sacred stream, Thy holy word,
Our grief allays, our fear controls;
Sweet peace Thy promises afford,
And give new strength to fainting souls.

5 Zion enjoys her Monarch's love,
Secure against a threatening hour;
Nor can her firm foundations move,
Built on His truth, and armed with power.

71

1 The Lord, how wondrous are His ways!
How firm His truth, how large His grace!
He takes His mercy for His throne;
And thence He makes His glories known.

2 Not half so high His power hath spread
The starry heavens, above our head,
As His rich love exceeds our praise—
Exceeds the highest hopes we raise.

3 Not half so far hath nature placed
The rising morning from the west,
As His forgiving grace removes
The daily guilt of those He loves.

4 His everlasting love is sure;
To all the saints it shall endure;
From age to age His truth shall reign,
Nor children's children hope in vain.

72

1 Eternal Spirit, we confess
And sing the wonders of Thy grace;
Thy power conveys our blessings down
From God the Father and the Son.

2 Enlightened by Thy heavenly ray,
Our shades and darkness turn to day;
Thine inward teachings make us know
Our danger and our refuge too.

3 The troubled conscience knows Thy voice,
Thy cheering words awake our joys;
Thy words allay the stormy wind,
And calm the surges of the mind.

73

1. When I survey the wondrous cross
On which the Prince of glory died,
My richest gain I count but loss,
And pour contempt on all my pride.

2. Forbid it, Lord, that I should boast,
Save in the death of Christ, my God;
All the vain things that charm me most,
I sacrifice them to His blood.

3. See, from His head, His hands, His feet,
Sorrow and love flow mingled down!
Did e'er such love and sorrow meet,
Or thorns compose so rich a crown?

4. Were the whole realm of nature mine,
That were a present far too small;
Love so amazing, so divine,
Demands my soul, my life, my all!

74

1. My dear Redeemer, and my Lord!
I read my duty in Thy word,
But in Thy life the law appears,
Drawn out in living characters.

2. Such was Thy truth, and such Thy zeal,
Such deference to Thy Father's will,
Such love and meekness so divine,
I would transcribe and make them mine.

3. Cold mountains, and the midnight air,
Witnessed the fervor of Thy prayer;
The desert Thy temptations knew,
Thy conflict, and Thy victory too.

4. Be Thou my pattern; make me bear
More of Thy gracious image here;
Then God, the Judge, shall own my name
Among the followers of the Lamb.

75

1. Sun of my soul, Thou Saviour dear,
It is not night if Thou be near;
O may no earth-born cloud arise
To hide Thee from Thy servant's eyes.

2. When the soft dews of kindly sleep
My wearied eyelids gently steep,
Be my last thought, how sweet to rest
Forever on my Saviour's breast.

3. Abide with me from morn till eve,
For without Thee I cannot live;
Abide with me when night is nigh,
For without Thee I dare not die.

4. Come near and bless us when we wake
Ere through the world our way we take,
Till in the ocean of Thy love
We lose ourselves in heaven above.

76

1. I love, I love Thee, Lord most high!
Because Thou first hast loved me;
I seek no other liberty
But that of being bound to Thee.

2. May memory no thought suggest,
But shall to Thy pure glory tend:
My understanding find no rest,
Except in Thee, its only end.

3. All mine is Thine; say but the word,
Whate'er Thou willest shall be done;
I know Thy love, all-gracious Lord;
I know it seeks my good alone.

4. Apart from Thee all things are naught;
Then grant, O my supremest Bliss,
Grant me to love Thee as I ought;
Thou givest all in giving this.

77

1. Father, in these reveal Thy Son,
In these for whom we seek Thy face;
Adopt and seal them as Thine own,
By Thy regenerating grace.

2. Jesus, with us Thou always art;
Now ratify the sacred sign,
The gift unspeakable impart,
And bless Thy sacrament divine.

3. Come, Holy Spirit, from on high,
Baptizer of our spirits, Thou!
The purifying grace apply,
And witness with the water now.

4. Pour forth Thine energy divine,
And sprinkle the atoning blood;
May Father, Son, and Spirit join
To seal each child a child of God.

78

1 Asleep in Jesus! blesséd sleep
From which none ever wakes to weep!
A calm and undisturbed repose,
Unbroken by the last of foes!

2 Asleep in Jesus! O how sweet
To be for such a slumber meet!
With holy confidence to sing
That death has lost his venomed sting!

3 Asleep in Jesus! peaceful rest
Whose waking is supremely blest!
No fear, no woe, shall dim that hour
That manifests the Saviour's power.

4 Asleep in Jesus! O for me
May such a blissful refuge be:
Securely shall my ashes lie,
And wait the summons from on high.

79

1 How blest the sacred tie that binds
In union sweet according minds;
How swift the heavenly course they run
Whose hearts, whose faith, whose hopes are one.

2 To each the soul of each how dear!
What jealous love, what holy fear!
How doth the generous flame within
Refine from earth and cleanse from sin!

3 Their streaming tears together flow
For human guilt and mortal woe;
Their ardent prayers together rise
Like mingling flames in sacrifice.

4 Nor shall the glowing flame expire
When nature droops her sickening fire;
Then shall they meet in realms above,
A heaven of joy, a heaven of love.

80

1 How sweet to leave the world awhile,
And seek the presence of our Lord!
Dear Saviour! on Thy people smile,
And come according to Thy word.

2 From busy scenes we now retreat,
That we may here converse with Thee;
Ah Lord! behold us at Thy feet;
Let this the "gate of heaven" be.

81

1 How blest the righteous when he dies,
When sinks a weary soul to rest!
How mildly beam the closing eyes,
How gently heaves the expiring breast!

2 So fades a summer cloud away;
So sinks the gale when storms are o'er;
So gently shuts the eye of day;
So dies a wave along the shore.

3 A holy quiet reigns around,
A calm which life nor death destroys;
Nothing disturbs that peace profound
Which his unfettered soul enjoys.

4 Life's labor done, as sinks the clay,
Light from its load the spirit flies,
While heaven and earth combine to say,
How blest the righteous when he dies!

82

1 Dear Saviour, if these lambs should stray
From Thy secure enclosure's bound,
And, lured by worldly joys away,
Among the thoughtless crowd be found,

2 Remember still that they are Thine,
That Thy dear sacred name they bear;
Think that the seal of love divine,
The sign of covenant grace, they wear.

3 In all their erring, sinful years,
O let them ne'er forgotten be!
Remember all the prayers and tears
Which made them consecrate to Thee.

4 And when these lips no more can pray,
These eyes can weep for them no more,
Turn Thou their feet from folly's way,
The wanderers to Thy fold restore.

83

1 Dismiss us with Thy blessing, Lord;
Help us to feed upon Thy word;
All that has been amiss forgive,
And let Thy truth within us live.

2 Though we are guilty, Thou art good;
Wash all our works in Jesus' blood;
Give every burdened soul release,
And bid us all depart in peace.

84
Psalm 51.

1 Show pity, Lord, O Lord, forgive;
Let a repenting rebel live;
Are not Thy mercies large and free!
May not a sinner trust in Thee!

2 My crimes are great, but don't surpass
The power and glory of Thy grace;
Great God, Thy nature hath no bound,
So let Thy pardoning love be found.

3 O wash my soul from every sin,
And make my guilty conscience clean!
Here on my heart the burden lies,
And past offences pain mine eyes.

4 My lips with shame my sins confess,
Against Thy law, against Thy grace;
Lord, should Thy judgment grow severe,
I am condemned, but Thou art clear.

5 Yet save a trembling sinner, Lord,
Whose hope, still hovering round Thy word,
Would light on some sweet promise there,
Some sure support against despair.

85

1 A broken heart, my God, my King,
Is all the sacrifice I bring;
The God of grace will ne'er despise
A broken heart for sacrifice.

2 My soul lies humbled in the dust,
And owns thy dreadful sentence just;
Look down, O Lord, with pitying eye,
And save the soul condemned to die.

3 Create my nature pure within,
And form my soul averse to sin,
Let Thy good Spirit ne'er depart,
Nor hide Thy presence from my heart.

4 Then will I teach the world Thy ways;
Sinners shall learn Thy sovereign grace,
I'll lead them to my Saviour's blood,
And they shall praise a pard'ning God.

86

1 O help us, Lord; each hour of need
Thy heavenly succor give;
Help us in thought, and word, and deed,
Each hour on earth we live.

2 O help us when our spirits bleed
With contrite anguish sore;
And when our hearts are cold and dead,
O help us, Lord, the more.

3 O help us through the prayer of faith
More firmly to believe;
For still the more the servant hath,
The more shall he receive.

4 O help us, Jesus, from on high;
We know no help but Thee;
O help us so to live and die
As Thine in heaven to be.

87

1 Behold a Stranger at the door!
He gently knocks, has knocked before,
Has waited long, is waiting still;
You treat no other friend so ill.

2 O lovely attitude! He stands
With melting heart and loaded hands!
O matchless kindness! and He shows
This matchless kindness to his foes!

3 Rise, touched with gratitude divine,
Turn out His enemy and thine,
That soul-destroying monster, Sin,
And let the Heavenly Stranger in.

4 Admit him, ere His anger burn;
His feet departed ne'er return;
Admit Him, or the hour's at hand,
When at His door denied you'll stand.

88
Psalm 69.

1 Deep in our hearts let us record
The deeper sorrows of our Lord,
Behold, the rising billows roll
To overwhelm His holy soul!

2 Yet, gracious God, Thy power and love
Have made the curse a blessing prove;
The dreadful sufferings of Thy Son
Atoned for sins which we had done.

3 O for His sake our guilt forgive,
And let the mourning sinner live!
The Lord will hear us in His name,
Nor shall our hope be turned to shame.

89

1 'Tis midnight; and on Olive's brow
The star is dimmed that lately shone:
'Tis midnight; in the garden now
The suffering Saviour prays alone.

2 'Tis midnight; and from all removed,
Immanuel wrestles lone with fears;
E'en the disciple that He loved
Heeds not His Master's grief and tears.

3 'Tis midnight; and for others' guilt
The Man of sorrows weeps in blood;
Yet He who hath in anguish knelt
Is not forsaken by His God.

4 'Tis midnight; and from ether-plains
Is borne the song that angels know;
Unheard by mortals are the strains
That sweetly soothe the Saviour's woe.

90

1 "'Tis finished!"—so the Saviour cried,
And meekly bowed His head, and died:
"'Tis finished!"—yes, the race is run,
The battle fought, the victory won.

2 'Tis finished!—all that heaven foretold
By prophets in the days of old;
And truths are opened to our view
That kings and prophets never knew.

3 'Tis finished!—Son of God, Thy power
Hath triumphed in this awful hour;
And yet our eyes with sorrow see
That life to us was death to Thee.

4 'Tis finished!—let the joyful sound
Be heard through all the nations round;
'Tis finished!—let the triumph rise
And swell the chorus of the skies.

91

1 That day of wrath! that dreadful day
When heaven and earth shall pass away!
What power shall be the sinner's stay!
How shall he meet that dreadful day,

2 When, shivering like a parchéd scroll,
The flaming heavens together roll;
When louder yet, and yet more dread,
Swells the high trump that wakes the dead!

3 O on that day, that wrathful day,
When man to judgment wakes from clay,
Be Thou the trembling sinner's stay,
Though heaven and earth shall pass away!

92

1 The Lord will come! the earth shall quake;
The hills their fixéd seat forsake;
And, withering, from the vault of night
The stars withdraw their feeble light.

2 The Lord will come! but not the same
As once in lowly form He came,
A silent Lamb to slaughter led,
The bruised, the suffering, and the dead.

3 The Lord will come! a dreadful form,
With wreath of flame, and robe of storm,
On cherub wings, and wings of wind,
Anointed Judge of human kind!

4 Can this be He, who wont to stray
A pilgrim on the world's highway,
By power oppressed, and mocked by pride,
The Nazarene, the Crucified!

5 While sinners in despair shall call,
"Rocks, hide us! mountains, on us fall!"
The saints, ascending from the tomb,
Shall sing for joy, "The Lord is come!"

93

1 Unveil thy bosom, faithful tomb!
Take this new treasure to thy trust,
And give these sacred relics room
To seek a slumber in the dust.

2 Nor pain, nor grief, nor anxious fear,
Invade thy bounds; no mortal woes
Can reach the peaceful sleeper here,
While angels watch the soft repose.

3 So Jesus slept; God's dying Son
Passed through the grave, and blessed the bed!
Rest here, blest saint! till, from His throne,
The morning break, and pierce the shade.

4 Break from His throne, illustrious morn!
Attend, O earth, His sovereign word!
Restore thy trust; a glorious form
Shall then arise to meet the Lord.

94
Psalm 146.

1 I'll praise my Maker with my breath;
And when my voice is lost in death,
Praise shall employ my nobler powers;
My days of praise shall ne'er be past
While life and thought and being last,
Or immortality endures.

2 Happy the man whose hopes rely
On Israel's God; He made the sky
And earth and seas with all their train;
His truth forever stands secure,
He saves the opprest, He feeds the poor,
And none shall find His promise vain.

3 He loves His saints, He knows them well;
But turns the wicked down to hell;
Thy God, O Zion! ever reigns;
Let every tongue, let every age,
In this exalted work engage:
Praise Him in everlasting strains.

4 I'll praise Him while He lends me breath;
And when my voice is lost in death,
Praise shall employ my nobler powers;
My days of praise shall ne'er be past
While life and thought and being last,
Or immortality endures.

95
Psalm 21.

1 Our Lord is risen from the dead;
Our Jesus is gone up on high;
The powers of hell are captive led,
Dragged to the portals of the sky.

2 There His triumphal chariot waits,
And angels chant the solemn lay;
Lift up your heads, ye heavenly gates!
Ye everlasting doors, give way!

3 Loose all your bars of massy light,
And wide unfold the ethereal scene;
He claims those mansions as His right;
Receive the King of glory in.

4 Who is the King of glory—who?
The Lord that all His foes o'ercame;
The world, sin, death, and hell o'erthrew;
And Jesus is the Conqueror's name.

5 Lo, His triumphal chariot waits,
And angels chant the solemn lay:
Lift up your heads, ye heavenly gates!
Ye everlasting doors give way!

6 Who is the King of glory—who?
The Lord of glorious power possest,
The King of saints and angels too,
God over all, forever blest.

96
Psalm 96.

1 Let all the earth their voices raise,
To sing the choicest psalm of praise;
To sing and bless Jehovah's name:
His glory let the heathen know;
His wonders to the nations show;
And all His saving works proclaim.

2 He framed the globe, He built the sky,
He made the shining worlds on high,
And reigns complete in glory there.
His beams are majesty and light;
His beauties, how divinely bright!
His temple, how divinely fair!

3 Come the great day, the glorious hour,
When earth shall feel His saving power,
And heathen nations fear His Name!
Then shall the race of man confess
The beauty of His holiness,
And in His courts His grace proclaim.

97

1 Thee we adore, eternal Lord!
We praise Thy name with one accord;
Thy saints, who here Thy goodness see;
Through all the world do worship Thee.

2 To Thee aloud all angels cry,
The heavens and all the powers on high;
Thee, holy, holy, holy King,
Lord God of hosts, they ever sing.

3 The apostles join the glorious throng;
The prophets swell the immortal song;
The martyrs' noble army raise
Eternal anthems to Thy praise.

4 From day to day, O Lord, do we
Highly exalt and honor Thee!
Thy name we worship and adore,
World without end, for evermore!

98
Psalm 23.

1 THE Lord my pasture shall prepare,
And feed me with a shepherd's care;
His presence shall my wants supply,
And guard me with a watchful eye;
My noonday walks He shall attend,
And all my midnight hours defend.

2 When in the sultry glebe I faint,
Or on the thirsty mountain pant,
To fertile vales and dewy meads
My weary, wandering steps he leads,
Where peaceful rivers, soft and slow,
Amid the verdant landscape flow.

3 Though in the paths of death I tread,
With gloomy horrors overspread,
My steadfast heart shall fear no ill,
For Thou, O Lord, art with me still;
Thy friendly rod shall give me aid,
And guide me through the dreadful shade.

99

1 CREATOR-SPIRIT, by whose aid
The world's foundations first were laid,
Come, visit every pious mind;
Come, pour Thy joys on human kind;
From sin and sorrow set us free,
And make Thy temples worthy Thee.

2 O Source of uncreated light!
The Father's promised Paraclete!
Thrice Holy Fount! Thrice Holy Fire!
Our hearts with heavenly love inspire!
Come, and Thy sacred unction bring
To sanctify us while we sing.

3 Immortal honor, endless fame
Attend the Almighty Father's name!
The Saviour-Son be glorified,
Who for lost man's redemption died!
And equal adoration be,
Eternal Paraclete, to Thee!

100

1 JESUS, Thy boundless love to me
No thought can reach, no tongue declare;
O knit my thankful heart to Thee,
And reign without a rival there;
Thine wholly, Thine alone, I am,
Be Thou alone my constant flame!

2 O Love, how cheering is Thy ray!
All pain before Thy presence flies;
Care, anguish, sorrow melt away
Where'er Thy healing beams arise;
O Jesus, nothing may I see,
Nothing desire or seek but Thee!

3 In suffering be Thy love my peace;
In weakness be Thy love my power;
And when the storms of life shall cease,
Jesus, in that important hour,
In death, as life, be Thou my Guide,
And save me, Who for me hast died.

101

1 COME, Holy Ghost, all-quickening fire,
Come, and in me delight to rest;
Grant the supplies that I require;
O come, and consecrate my breast;
The temple of my soul prepare,
And fix Thy sacred presence there.

2 My peace, my life, my comfort Thou,
My treasure and my all Thou art;
True Witness of my sonship now,
Engraving Christ upon my heart,
Seal of my sins in Him forgiven,
Earnest of love, and pledge of heaven.

102

1 WHEN gathering clouds around I view,
And days are dark, and friends are few,
On Him I lean who, not in vain,
Experienced every human pain;
He sees my wants, allays my fears,
And counts and treasures up my tears.

2 If aught should tempt my soul to stray
From heavenly virtue's narrow way;
To fly the good I would pursue,
Or do the sin I would not do;
Still He, who felt temptation's power,
Shall guard me in that dangerous hour.

3 And, O! when I have safely past
Through every conflict but the last,
Still, still unchanging, watch beside
My painful bed, for Thou hast died!
Then point to realms of cloudless day,
And wipe my latest tear away.

103

1 Sweet Saviour, bless us ere we go;
Thy word into our minds instil;
And make our lukewarm hearts to glow
With lowly love and fervent will.
Through life's long day and death's dark night,
O gentle Jesus, be our light.

2 Grant us, dear Lord, from evil ways
True absolution and release;
And bless us, more than in past days,
With purity and inward peace.
Through life's long day and death's dark night,
O gentle Jesus, be our light.

3 Do more than pardon; give us joy,
Sweet fear, and sober liberty,
And simple hearts without alloy,
That only long to be like Thee.
Through life's long day and death's dark night,
O gentle Jesus, be our light.

4 For all we love, the poor, the sad,
The sinful, unto Thee we call;
O let Thy mercy make us glad!
Thou art our Jesus, and our all.
Through life's long day and death's dark night,
O gentle Jesus, be our light.

104

1 Jesus, my Lord, my God, my All,
Hear me, blest Saviour, when I call;
Hear me, and from Thy dwelling-place
Pour down the riches of Thy grace.
Jesus, my Lord, I Thee adore;
O make me love Thee more and more!

2 Jesus, too late I Thee have sought;
How can I love Thee as I ought!
And how extol Thy matchless fame,
The glorious beauty of Thy Name!

3 Jesus, what didst Thou find in me
That Thou hast dealt so lovingly?
How great the joy that Thou hast brought,
So far exceeding hope or thought!

4 Jesus, of Thee shall be my song,
To Thee my heart and soul belong;
All that I have or am is Thine,
And Thou, blest Saviour, Thou art mine.

105

1 Like Israel's host to exile driven,
Across the flood the fathers fled;
Their hands bore up the ark of heaven,
And heaven their trusting footsteps led,
Till on these savage shores they trod,
And won the wilderness for God.

2 Then, when their weary ark found rest,
Another Zion proudly grew,
In more than Judah's glory dressed,
With light that Israel never knew:
From sea to sea her empire spread,
Her temple heaven, and Christ her Head.

3 Then let the grateful church, to-day,
Her ancient rite with gladness keep;
And still our fathers' God display
His kindness, though the fathers sleep.
O bless as thou hast blessed the past,
While earth, and time, and heaven shall last!

106

1 When streaming from the eastern skies,
The morning light salutes mine eyes,
O Sun of righteousness divine,
On me with beams of mercy shine;
O chase the shades of guilt away,
And turn my darkness into day.

2 And when to heaven's all-glorious King
My morning sacrifice I bring,
And mourning o'er my guilt and shame,
Ask mercy in my Saviour's name;
Then, Jesus, cleanse me with Thy blood,
And be my Advocate with God.

3 When each day's scenes and labors close,
And wearied nature seeks repose,
With pardoning mercy richly blest,
Guard me, my Saviour, while I rest;
And as each morning's sun shall rise,
O lead me onward to the skies!

AMES. L. M.

RETREAT. L. M.

FOREST. L. M.

LOVING KINDNESS. L. M.

107
Psalm 87. [Ames.]

1 God in His earthly temples lays
Foundations for His heavenly praise,
He likes the tents of Jacob well;
But still in Zion loves to dwell.

2 His mercy visits every house,
That pays its night and morning vows;
But makes a more delightful stay,
Where churches meet to praise and pray.

3 What glories were described of old!
What wonders are of Zion told!
Thou city of our God below,
Thy fame shall Tyre and Egypt know.

4 When God makes up His last account
Of natives in His holy mount,
'Twill be an honor to appear,
As one new born and nourished there.

108
Psalm 68. [Ames.]

1 Kingdoms and thrones to God belong;
Crown Him, ye nations, in your song:
His wondrous names and powers rehearse;
His honors shall enrich your verse.

2 He shakes the heavens with loud alarms;
How terrible is God in arms!
In Israel are His mercies known,
Israel is His peculiar throne.

3 Proclaim Him King, pronounce Him blest;
He's your defence, your joy, your rest;
When terrors rise, and nations faint,
God is the strength of every saint.

109
[Retreat.]

1 From every stormy wind that blows,
From every swelling tide of woes,
There is a calm, a sure retreat;
'Tis found beneath the mercy-seat.

2 There is a place where Jesus sheds
The oil of gladness on our heads,
A place than all besides more sweet;
It is the blood-bought mercy-seat.

3 There is a scene where spirits blend,
Where friend holds fellowship with friend;
Though sundered far, by faith they meet
Around one common mercy-seat.

4 O let my hand forget her skill,
My tongue be silent, cold, and still,
This throbbing heart forget to beat,
If I forget the mercy-seat!

110
[Forest.]

1 Jesus, my All, to Heaven is gone,
He that I placed my hopes upon;
His track I see, and I'll pursue
The narrow way till Him I view.

2 This is the way I long have sought,
And mourned because I found it not;
My grief, my burden, long have been
Because I could not cease from sin.

3 The more I strove against its power,
I sinned and stumbled but the more;
Till late I heard my Saviour say,
"Come hither, soul! I am the Way!"

4 Lo! glad I come; and Thou, dear Lamb,
Shalt take me to Thee, as I am:
Nothing but sin I Thee can give;
Yet help me, and Thy praise I'll live!

111
[Loving-Kindness.]

1 Awake, my soul, in joyful lays,
And sing thy great Redeemer's praise;
He justly claims a song from me:
His loving-kindness, O how free!

2 He saw me ruined in the fall,
Yet loved me notwithstanding all;
He saved me from my lost estate;
His loving-kindness, O how great!

3 When trouble, like a gloomy cloud,
Has gathered thick and thundered loud,
He near my soul has always stood:
His loving-kindness, O how good!

4 Often I feel my sinful heart
Prone from my Jesus to depart;
But though I have Him oft forgot,
His loving-kindness changes not.

5 Soon shall I pass the gloomy vale;
Soon all my mortal powers must fail;
O may my last expiring breath
His loving-kindness sing in death!

CHRISTIAN PRAISE.

SWANWICK. C. M.

DEWITT. C. M.

BRADFORD. C. M.

112

1 The Lord our God is full of might,
The winds obey His will;
He speaks, and in His heavenly height
The rolling sun stands still.

2 Rebel, ye waves, and o'er the land
With threatening aspect roar;
The Lord uplifts His awful hand,
And chains you to the shore.

3 Ye winds of night, your force combine;
Without His high behest,
Ye shall not in the mountain pine
Disturb the sparrow's nest.

4 His voice sublime is heard afar,
In distant peals it dies;
He yokes the whirlwind to His car,
And sweeps the howling skies.

5 Ye nations, bend, in reverence bend,
Ye monarchs, wait His nod,
And bid the choral song ascend
To celebrate your God.

113
Psalm 18.

1 The Lord descended from above
And bowed the heavens most high,
And underneath His feet He cast
The darkness of the sky.

2 On cherub and on cherubim
Full royally He rode,
And on the wings of mighty winds
Came flying all abroad.

3 He sat serene upon the floods,
Their fury to restrain;
And He, as sovereign Lord and King,
For evermore shall reign.

4 Give glory to His holy name,
And honor Him alone;
Give worship to His majesty,
Upon His holy throne.

114

1 Great God! how infinite art Thou!
What worthless worms are we!
Let the whole race of creatures bow,
And pay their praise to Thee.

2 Thy throne eternal ages stood,
Ere seas or stars were made;
Thou art the ever-living God,
Were all the nations dead.

3 Eternity, with all its years,
Stands present in Thy view;
To Thee there's nothing old appears,
Great God! there's nothing new.

4 Our lives through various scenes are drawn,
And vexed with trifling cares;
While Thine eternal thought moves on
Thine undisturbed affairs.

115

1 God moves in a mysterious way
His wonders to perform;
He plants His footsteps in the sea,
And rides upon the storm.

2 Deep in unfathomable mines
Of never-failing skill,
He treasures up His bright designs,
And works His sovereign will.

3 Ye fearful saints, fresh courage take;
The clouds ye so much dread
Are big with mercy, and shall break
In blessings on your head.

4 Judge not the Lord by feeble sense,
But trust Him for His grace;
Behind a frowning providence,
He hides a smiling face.

116

1 Keep silence, all created things,
And wait your Maker's nod!
My soul stands trembling while she sings
The honors of her God.

2 Life, death, and hell, and worlds unknown
Hang on His firm decree;
He sits on no precarious throne,
Nor borrows leave to be.

3 Chained to His throne a volume lies,
With all the fates of men;
With every angel's form and size,
Drawn by the eternal pen.

4 His providence unfolds the book,
And makes His counsels shine;
Each opening leaf, and every stroke,
Fulfils some deep design.

5 In Thy fair book of life and grace,
O may I find my name,
Recorded in some humble place
Beneath my Lord, the Lamb.

117

1. All hail the power of Jesus' Name!
 Let | angels prostrate | fall;
 Bring forth the royal diadem,
 And | crown Him | Lord of | all!

2. Crown Him, ye morning-stars of light
 Who | fixed this floating | ball;
 Now hail the strength of Israel's might,
 And | crown Him | Lord of | all!

3. Crown Him, ye martyrs of our God,
 Who | from His altar | call;
 Extol the stem of Jesse's rod,
 And | crown Him | Lord of | all!

4. Hail Him, ye heirs of David's line,
 Whom | David Lord did | call;
 The God Incarnate, Man Divine,
 And | crown Him | Lord of | all!

5. Sinners, whose love can ne'er forget
 The | wormwood and the | gall,
 Go spread your trophies at His feet,
 And | crown Him | Lord of | all!

6. Let every kindred, every tribe,
 On | this terrestrial | ball,
 To Him all majesty ascribe,
 And | crown Him | Lord of | all!

118

1. Arise, ye people! and adore,
 Exulting strike the chord;
 Let all the earth, from shore to shore,
 Confess the Almighty Lord.

2. Glad shouts aloud, wide echoing round,
 The ascending God proclaim;
 The angelic choir respond the sound,
 And shake creation's frame.

3. They sing of death and hell o'erthrown
 In that triumphant hour;
 And God exalts His conquering Son
 To His right hand of power.

119 Psalm 45.

1. Jesus, immortal King! arise;
 Rise and assert Thy sway;
 Till earth, subdued, its tribute bring,
 And distant lands obey.

2. Ride forth, victorious Conqueror, ride,
 Till all Thy foes submit;
 And all the powers of hell resign
 Their trophies at Thy feet.

3. Send forth Thy word, and let it fly
 This spacious earth around;
 Till every soul beneath the sun
 Shall hear the joyful sound.

4. From sea to sea, from shore to shore,
 May Jesus be adored;
 And earth, with all her millions, shout
 Hosannas to the Lord.

120

1. This is the day the Lord hath made,
 He calls the hours His own;
 Let heaven rejoice, let earth be glad,
 And praise surround the throne.

2. To-day He rose and left the dead,
 And Satan's empire fell;
 To-day the saints His triumph spread,
 And all His wonders tell.

3. Hosanna to the anointed King,
 To David's holy Son:
 Help us, O Lord! descend and bring
 Salvation from Thy throne.

4. Hosanna, in the highest strains
 The church on earth can raise;
 The highest heavens, in which He reigns,
 Shall give Him nobler praise.

121

1. The whole creation groans, and waits,
 Till we who love Thee, Lord,
 Shall stand within Thy temple gates,
 And shine, the sons of God.

2. The sons of God, how bright they shine!
 No mortal eye can see;
 We sinners shall be made divine;
 We shall be one with Thee.

3. One with the Lord and all His saints,
 Thy nature in our own,
 Thy crown our rich inheritance,
 Heirs to Thy royal throne!

122
Psalm 98.

1 Joy to the world! the Lord is come!
Let earth receive her King;
Let every heart prepare Him room,
And heaven and nature sing.

2 Joy to the world! the Saviour reigns!
Let men their songs employ;
While fields and floods, rocks, hills, and plains
Repeat the sounding joy.

3 No more let sin and sorrow grow,
Nor thorns infest the ground;
He comes to make His blessings flow
Far as the curse is found.

4 He rules the world with truth and grace,
And makes the nations prove
The glories of His righteousness,
And wonders of His love.

123
Psalm 96.

1 Sing to the Lord, ye distant lands,
Ye tribes of every tongue!
His rich display of grace demands
A new and nobler song.

2 Say to the nations, Jesus reigns,
God's own almighty Son;
His power the sinking world sustains
And grace surrounds His throne.

3 Let heaven proclaim the joyful day,
Joy through the earth be seen;
Let cities shine in bright array,
And fields in cheerful green.

4 Let an unusual joy surprise
The islands of the sea;
Ye mountains sink, ye valleys rise,
Prepare the Lord His way.

5 Behold, He comes! He comes to bless
The nations as their God;
To show the world His righteousness,
And send His truth abroad.

124

1 Lo, what a glorious sight appears
To our believing eyes!
The earth and seas are passed away,
And the old rolling skies.

2 From the third heaven, where God resides,
That holy, happy place,
The New Jerusalem comes down,
Adorned with shining grace.

3 Attending angels shout for joy,
And the bright armies sing,
"Mortals, behold the sacred seat
Of your descending King.

4 "The God of glory, down to men,
Removes His blest abode;
Men, the dear objects of His grace,
And He their loving God."

5 How long, dear Saviour, O how long
Shall this bright hour delay!
Fly swifter round, ye wheels of time,
And bring the welcome day.

125

1 Come, let us join our cheerful songs,
With angels round the throne;
Ten thousand thousand are their tongues,
But all their joys are one.

2 "Worthy the Lamb that died," they cry,
"To be exalted thus!"
"Worthy the Lamb," our lips reply,
"For He was slain for us!"

3 Jesus is worthy to receive
Honor and power divine;
And blessings, more than we can give,
Be, Lord, forever Thine.

4 Let all who dwell above the sky,
And air, and earth, and seas
Conspire to lift Thy glories high,
And speak Thine endless praise.

5 The whole creation join in one,
To bless the sacred name
Of Him who sits upon the throne,
And to adore the Lamb.

DOXOLOGY.

To Father, Son, and Holy Ghost,
The God whom we adore;
Be glory, as it was, is now,
And shall be evermore.

126

1 Come, let us join our friends above
That have obtained the prize;
And on the eagle wings of love,
To joys celestial rise.

2 Let all the saints terrestrial sing
With those to glory gone:
For all the servants of our King,
In heaven and earth, are one.

3 One family, we dwell in Him,
One church above, beneath,
Though now divided by the stream,
The narrow stream of death.

4 One army of the living God,
To His command we bow;
Part of His host have crossed the flood,
And part are crossing now.

5 His militant, embodied host,
With wishful looks we stand,
And long to see that happy coast,
And reach the heavenly land.

127

1 Awake, my soul! stretch every nerve,
And press with vigor on;
A heavenly race demands thy zeal,
And an immortal crown.

2 A cloud of witnesses around
Hold thee in full survey;
Forget the steps already trod,
And onward urge thy way.

3 'Tis God's all-animating voice,
That calls thee from on high;
'Tis His own hand presents the prize
To thine aspiring eye.

4 Blest Saviour, introduced by Thee,
Have I my race begun;
And, crowned with victory, at Thy feet
I'll lay my honors down.

128

1 To us a Child of hope is born,
To us a Son is given;
Him shall the tribes of earth obey,
Him all the hosts of heaven.

2 His name shall be the Prince of Peace,
For evermore adored;
The Wonderful, the Counsellor,
The great and mighty Lord!

3 His power, increasing, still shall spread;
His reign no end shall know;
Justice shall guard His throne above,
And peace abound below.

4 To us a Child of hope is born,
To us a Son is given;
The Wonderful, the Counsellor,
The mighty Lord of heaven.

129

1 Salvation! O the joyful sound!
'Tis pleasure to our ears;
A sovereign balm for every wound,
A cordial for our fears.

2 Buried in sorrow and in sin,
At hell's dark door we lay;
But we arise by grace divine
To see a heavenly day.

3 Salvation! let the echo fly
The spacious earth around;
While all the armies of the sky
Conspire to raise the sound.

130

1 Light of the lonely pilgrim's heart,
Star of the coming day!
Arise, and with Thy morning beams
Chase all our griefs away!

2 Come, blessèd Lord, let every shore
And answering island sing
The praises of Thy royal name,
And own Thee as their King.

3 Bid the whole earth, responsive now
To the bright world above,
Break forth in sweetest strains of joy,
In memory of Thy love.

4 Thine was the cross, with all its fruits
Of grace and peace divine;
Be Thine the crown of glory now,
The palm of victory Thine!

131

1 The eternal gates lift up their heads,
The doors are opened wide;
The King of glory is gone up
Unto His Father's side.

2 Thou art gone in before us, Lord,
Thou hast prepared a place,
That we may be where now Thou art,
And look upon Thy face.

3 And ever on Thine earthly path
A gleam of glory lies;
A light still breaks behind the cloud
That veils Thee from our eyes.

4 Lift up our thoughts, lift up our songs,
And let Thy grace be given,
That, while we linger yet below,
Our hearts may be in heaven:

5 That where Thou art at God's right hand,
Our hope, our love may be:
Dwell in us now, that we may dwell
For evermore in Thee.

132 Psalm 27.

1 The Lord of Glory is my light,
And my salvation too;
God is my strength, nor will I fear
What all my foes can do.

2 One privilege my heart desires:
O grant me an abode
Among the churches of Thy saints,
The temples of my God.

3 There shall I offer my requests,
And see Thy beauty still;
Shall hear Thy messages of love,
And there inquire Thy will.

4 When troubles rise, and storms appear,
There may His children hide;
God has a strong pavilion where
He makes my soul abide.

5 Now shall my head be lifted high
Above my foes around,
And songs of joy and victory
Within Thy temple sound.

133

1 Hark, the glad sound! the Saviour comes,
The Saviour promised long;
Let every heart prepare a throne,
And every voice a song.

2 He comes the prisoner to release,
In Satan's bondage held;
The gates of brass before Him burst,
The iron fetters yield.

3 He comes, from thickest films of vice
To clear the mental ray,
And on the eyeballs of the blind
To pour celestial day.

4 He comes the broken heart to bind,
The bleeding soul to cure,
And with the treasures of His grace
Enrich the humble poor.

5 Our glad hosannas, Prince of Peace,
Thy welcome shall proclaim,
And heaven's eternal arches ring
With Thy belovéd name.

134

1 With joy we hail the sacred day,
Which God has called His own;
With joy the summons we obey
To worship at His throne.

2 Thy chosen temple, Lord, how fair!
Where willing votaries throng,
To breathe the humble, fervent prayer,
And pour the choral song.

3 Spirit of grace! O deign to dwell
Within Thy church below;
Make her in holiness excel,
With pure devotion glow.

4 Let peace within her walls be found;
Let all her sons unite
To spread, with grateful zeal, around
Her clear and shining light.

5 Great God! we hail the sacred day,
Which Thou hast called Thine own;
With joy the summons we obey
To worship at Thy throne.

135
Psalm 69.

1 My never-ceasing song shall show
The mercies of the Lord;
And make succeeding ages know
How faithful is His word.

2 The sacred truths His lips pronounce
Shall firm as heaven endure;
And if He speaks a promise once,
Th' eternal grace is sure.

3 How long the race of David held
The promised Jewish throne;
But there's a nobler covenant sealed
To David's greater Son.

4 Lord God of hosts! Thy wondrous ways
Are sung by saints above;
And saints on earth their honors raise
To Thine unchanging love.

136

1 O FOR a thousand tongues to sing
My dear Redeemer's praise,
The glories of my God and King,
The triumphs of His grace!

2 My gracious Master and my God,
Assist me to proclaim,
To spread through all the earth abroad
The honors of Thy name.

3 Jesus! the name that charms our fears,
That bids our sorrows cease;
'Tis music in the sinner's ears,
'Tis life, and health, and peace.

4 He breaks the power of cancelled sin,
He sets the prisoner free;
His blood can make the foulest clean,
His blood avails for me.

137
Psalm 67.

1 SHINE on our land, Jehovah, shine
With beams of heavenly grace;
Reveal Thy power through all our coasts,
And show Thy smiling face.

2 Here fix Thy throne exalted high,
And here our glory stand;
And, like a wall of guardian fire,
Surround Thy favorite land.

3 When shall Thy name from shore to shore
Sound all the earth abroad;
And distant nations know and love
Their Saviour and their God!

4 Sing to the Lord, ye distant lands,
Sing loud with solemn voice;
Let thankful tongues exalt His praise,
And thankful hearts rejoice.

138

1 GIVE me the wings of faith to rise
Within the veil, and see
The saints above, how great their joys,
How bright their glories be.

2 I ask them whence their victory came;
They, with united breath,
Ascribe their conquest to the Lamb,
Their triumph to His death.

3 They marked the footsteps that He trod,
His zeal inspired their breast;
And, following their incarnate God,
Possess the promised rest.

4 Our glorious Leader claims our praise,
For His own pattern given;
While the long cloud of witnesses
Show the same path to heaven.

139
Psalm 132.

1 ARISE, O King of grace, arise,
And enter to Thy rest;
Lo, Thy church waits, with longing eyes,
Thus to be owned and blest!

2 Enter with all Thy glorious train,
Thy Spirit and Thy word;
All that the ark did once contain,
Could no such grace afford.

3 Here let the Son of David reign,
Let God's Anointed shine;
Justice and truth His court maintain,
With love and power divine.

4 Here let Him hold a lasting throne,
And as His kingdom grows,
Fresh honors shall adorn His crown,
And shame confound His foes.

140

1 I've found the pearl of greatest price,
My heart doth sing for joy;
And sing I must, for Christ is mine!
Christ shall my song employ.

2 Christ is my prophet, priest, and king:
My prophet full of light;
My great high-priest before the throne,
My king of heavenly might.

3 For He indeed is Lord of lords,
And He the King of kings;
He is the Son of righteousness,
With healing in His wings.

4 Christ Jesus is my all in all,
My comfort and my love;
My life below, and He shall be
My joy and crown above.

141

1 The morning purples all the sky,
The air with praises rings;
Defeated hell stands sullen by,
The world exulting sings:

2 While He, the King all strong to save,
Rends the dark doors away;
And through the breaches of the grave
Strides forth into the day.

3 The shining angels cry, "Away
With grief, no spices bring;
Not tears but songs, this joyful day,
Should greet the rising King.

4 That Thou our Paschal Lamb may'st be,
And endless joy begin,
Jesus, deliverer, set us free
From the dread death of sin.

5 Glory to God! our glad lips cry;
All praise and worship be
On earth, in heaven, to God most high,
For Christ's great victory!

142
Psalm 145.

1 Long as I live I'll bless Thy name,
My King! my God of love!
My work and joy shall be the same
In the bright world above.

2 Great is the Lord, His power unknown,
And let His praise be great;
I'll sing the honors of Thy throne,
Thy works of grace repeat.

3 Thy grace shall dwell upon my tongue
And, while my lips rejoice,
The men who hear my sacred song
Shall join their cheerful voice.

4 Fathers to sons shall teach Thy name,
And children learn Thy ways;
Ages to come Thy truth proclaim,
And nations sound Thy praise.

143

1 Come, ye that love the Saviour's name,
And joy to make it known;
The Sovereign of your hearts proclaim,
And bow before His throne.

2 Behold your King, your Saviour crowned
With glories all divine!
And tell the wond'ring nations round,
How bright those glories shine.

3 When in His earthly courts we view
The glories of our King,
We long to love as angels do,
And wish, like them, to sing.

4 O happy period! glorious day!
When heav'n and earth shall raise,
With all their pow'rs, th' enraptured lay,
To celebrate Thy praise.

144

1 How happy every child of grace,
Who knows his sins forgiven;
This earth, he cries, is not my place,
I seek my place in heaven.

2 A country far from mortal sight,
Yet, O, by faith, I see;
The land of rest, the saint's delight,
The heaven prepared for me.

3 We feel the resurrection near,
Our life in Christ concealed;
And with His glorious presence here,
Our earthen vessels filled.

4 O what a blessèd hope is ours!
While here on earth we stay;
We more than taste the heavenly powers,
And ante-date that day.

145   Psalm 71.

1 My Saviour, my Almighty Friend,
  When I begin Thy praise,
Where will the growing numbers end,
  The numbers of Thy grace!

2 Thou art my everlasting trust,
  Thy goodness I adore;
And since I knew Thy graces first,
  I speak Thy glories more.

3 My feet shall travel all the length
  Of the celestial road;
And march with courage in Thy strength
  To see my Father, God.

4 How will my lips rejoice to tell
  The victories of my King!
My soul, redeemed from sin and hell,
  Shall Thy salvation sing.

5 Awake, awake, my tuneful powers!
  With this delightful song
I'll entertain the darkest hours,
  Nor think the season long.

146   Psalm 122.

1 How did my heart rejoice to hear
  My friends devoutly say,
"In Zion let us all appear,
  And keep the solemn day."

2 I love her gates, I love the road;
  The church, adorned with grace,
Stands like a palace built for God,
  To show His milder face.

3 Up to her courts, with joys unknown,
  The holy tribes repair;
The Son of David holds His throne
  And sits in judgment there.

4 Peace be within this sacred place,
  And joy a constant guest;
With holy gifts and heavenly grace
  Be her attendants blest.

5 My soul shall pray for Zion still,
  While life or breath remains;
Here my best friends, my kindred dwell,
  Here God my Saviour reigns.

147   Psalm 5.

1 LORD! in the morning Thou shalt hear
  My voice ascending high;
To Thee will I direct my prayer,
  To Thee lift up mine eye:

2 Up to the hills where Christ is gone
  To plead for all His saints,
Presenting at His Father's throne
  Our songs and our complaints.

3 Thou art a God before whose sight
  The wicked shall not stand;
Sinners shall ne'er be Thy delight,
  Nor dwell at Thy right hand.

4 But to Thy house will I resort,
  To taste Thy mercies there;
I will frequent Thy holy court,
  And worship in Thy fear.

5 O may Thy Spirit guide my feet
  In ways of righteousness,
Make every path of duty straight
  And plain before my face.

148   Psalm 116.

1 WHAT shall I render to my God
  For all His kindness shown?
My feet shall visit Thine abode,
  My songs address Thy throne.

2 Among the saints that fill Thy house,
  My offerings shall be paid;
There shall my zeal perform the vows
  My soul in anguish made.

3 How much is mercy Thy delight,
  Thou ever blesséd God!
How dear Thy servants in Thy sight,
  How precious is their blood!

4 How happy all Thy servants are,
  How great Thy grace to me!
My life, which Thou hast made Thy care,
  Lord, I devote to Thee.

5 Now I am Thine, forever Thine,
  Nor shall my purpose move;
Thy hand hath loosed my bonds of pain,
  And bound me with Thy love.

149   Psalm 90.

1 Our God, our help in ages past,
Our hope for years to come,
Our shelter from the stormy blast,
And our eternal home:

2 Beneath the shadow of Thy throne
Thy saints have dwelt secure;
Sufficient is Thine arm alone,
And our defence is sure.

3 Before the hills in order stood,
Or earth received her frame;
From everlasting Thou art God—
To endless years the same.

4 Our God! our help in ages past,
Our hope for years to come,
Be Thou our guard while troubles last,
And our eternal home.

150   Psalm 73.

1 God! my supporter and my hope,
My help forever near,
Thine arm of mercy held me up
When sinking in despair.

2 Thy counsels, Lord, shall guide my feet
Through this dark wilderness;
Thy hand conduct me near Thy seat,
To dwell before Thy face.

3 Were I in heaven without my God,
'Twould be no joy to me;
And while this earth is my abode,
I long for none but Thee.

4 What if the springs of life were broke,
And flesh and heart should faint:
God is my soul's eternal rock,
The strength of every saint.

151

1 O Jesus, King most wonderful,
Thou Conqueror renowned!
Thou sweetness most ineffable,
In whom all joys are found!

2 O Jesus, light of all below!
Thou fount of life and fire!
Surpassing all the joys we know,
All that we can desire!

3 May every heart confess Thy name,
And ever Thee adore;
And seeking Thee, itself inflame
To seek Thee more and more.

4 Thee may our tongues forever bless;
Thee may we love alone;
And ever in our life express
The image of Thine own.

152

1 My God, how wonderful Thou art,
Thy majesty how bright!
How beautiful Thy mercy-seat
In depths of burning light!

2 How dread are Thine eternal years,
O everlasting Lord!
By prostrate spirits day and night
Incessantly adored.

3 How wonderful, how beautiful,
The sight of Thee must be,
Thine endless wisdom, boundless power,
And awful purity!

4 Father of Jesus, love's reward,
What rapture will it be,
Prostrate before Thy throne to lie,
And ever gaze on Thee!

153   Psalm 121.

1 To Zion's hill I lift mine eyes,
From thence expecting aid;
From Zion's hill, and Zion's God
Who heaven and earth has made.

2 Thou, then, my soul, in safety rest;
Thy Guardian will not sleep;
His watchful care that Israel guards,
Will thee in safety keep.

3 Sheltered beneath the Almighty's wings,
Thou shalt securely rest,
Where neither sun nor moon shall thee
By day or night molest.

4 At home, abroad, in peace, in war,
Thy God shall thee defend,
Conduct thee through life's pilgrimage
Safe to thy journey's end.

154

1 I'm not ashamed to own my Lord,
Or to defend His cause;
Maintain the honor of His word,
The glory of His cross.

2 Jesus, my God, I know His Name,
His Name is all my trust;
Nor will He put my soul to shame,
Nor let my hope be lost.

3 Firm as His throne His promise stands,
And He can well secure
What I've committed to His hands,
Till the decisive hour.

4 Then will He own my worthless name,
Before His Father's face,
And, in the New Jerusalem,
Appoint my soul a place.

155

1 A GLORY gilds the sacred page,
Majestic like the sun;
It gives a light to every age;
It gives, but borrows none.

2 The hand that gave it still supplies
The gracious light and heat;
His truths upon the nations rise;
They rise, but never set.

3 Let everlasting thanks be Thine,
For such a bright display,
As makes a world of darkness shine
With beams of heavenly day.

4 My soul rejoices to pursue
The steps of Him I love,
Till glory break upon my view
In brighter worlds above.

156

1 O JESUS, Thou the beauty art
Of angel-worlds above;
Thy name is music to the heart,
Enchanting it with love.

2 O Jesus, Saviour, hear the sighs
Which unto Thee I send;
To Thee my inmost spirit cries,
My being's hope and end.

3 Stay with us, Lord, and with Thy light
Illume the soul's abyss;
Scatter the darkness of our night,
And fill the world with bliss.

4 O Jesus, King of earth and heaven,
Our life and joy, to Thee
Be honor, thanks, and blessing given,
Through all eternity.

157

1 AM I a soldier of the cross,
A follower of the Lamb,
And shall I fear to own His cause,
Or blush to speak His name!

2 Are there no foes for me to face?
Must I not stem the flood?
Is this vile world a friend to grace
To help me on to God?

3 Sure I must fight, if I would reign;
Increase my courage, Lord;
I'll bear the toil, endure the pain,
Supported by Thy word.

4 Thy saints, in all this glorious war,
Shall conquer, though they die;
They see the triumph from afar,
And seize it with their eye.

5 When that illustrious day shall rise,
And all Thine armies shine,
In robes of victory through the skies
The glory shall be Thine.

158

1 IN all my Lord's appointed ways
My journey I'll pursue;
Hinder me not, ye much-loved saints,
For I must go with you.

2 Through floods and flames, if Jesus lead,
I'll follow where He goes;
Hinder me not! shall be my cry,
Though earth and hell oppose.

3 Through duty and through trials too,
I'll go at His command;
Hinder me not, for I am bound
To my Immanuel's land.

159

1 There is a land of pure delight,
Where saints immortal reign,
Infinite day excludes the night,
And pleasures banish pain.

2 There everlasting spring abides,
And never-withering flowers;
Death, like a narrow sea, divides
This heavenly land from ours.

3 Sweet fields, beyond the swelling flood,
Stand dressed in living green;
So to the Jews old Canaan stood,
While Jordan rolled between.

4 O could we make our doubts remove,
Those gloomy doubts that rise,
And see the Canaan that we love
With unbeclouded eyes:

5 Could we but climb where Moses stood,
And view the landscape o'er,
Not Jordan's stream, nor death's cold flood,
Should fright us from the shore.

160

1 O mother dear, Jerusalem,
When shall I come to thee!
When shall my sorrows have an end,
Thy joys when shall I see!

2 O happy harbor of God's saints!
O sweet and pleasant soil!
In thee no sorrow can be found,
Nor grief, nor care, nor toil.

3 Right through thy streets, with pleasing sound
The flood of life doth flow,
And on the banks, on either side,
The trees of life do grow:

4 Those trees each month yield ripened fruit,
For evermore they spring;
And all the nations of the earth
To thee their honors bring.

5 No dimming cloud o'ershadows thee,
Nor gloom, nor darksome night;
But every soul shines as the sun,
For God Himself gives light.

6 O mother dear, Jerusalem!
When shall I come to thee!
When shall my sorrows have an end!
Thy joys when shall I see!

161

1 Jerusalem, my happy home,
Name ever dear to me!
When shall my labors have an end
In joy and peace in thee!

2 When shall these eyes thy heaven-built walls
And pearly gates behold!
Thy bulwarks with salvation strong,
And streets of shining gold!

3 O when, thou city of my God,
Shall I thy courts ascend,
Where congregations ne'er break up,
And Sabbaths have no end!

4 There happier bowers than Eden's bloom,
Nor sin nor sorrow know:
Blest seats! through rude and stormy scenes,
I onward press to you.

5 Jerusalem, my happy home!
My soul still pants for thee;
Then shall my labors have an end,
When I thy joys shall see.

162

1 When I can read my title clear
To mansions in the skies,
I bid farewell to every fear,
And wipe my weeping eyes.

2 Should earth against my soul engage,
And hellish darts be hurled,
Then I can smile at Satan's rage,
And face a frowning world.

3 Let cares like a wild deluge come,
And storms of sorrow fall,
May I but safely reach my home,
My God, my heaven, my all!

4 There shall I bathe my weary soul
In seas of heavenly rest,
And not a wave of trouble roll
Across my peaceful breast.

163

1. While shepherds watched their flocks by night,
All seated on the ground,
The angel of the Lord came down,
And glory shone around.

2. "Fear not," said he—for mighty dread
Had seized their troubled mind—
"Glad tidings of great joy I bring
To you and all mankind.

3. "To you, in David's town, this day,
Is born of David's line,
The Saviour who is Christ, the Lord;
And this shall be the sign:

4. The heavenly Babe you there shall find
To human view displayed,
All meanly wrapped in swathing bands,
And in a manger laid."

5. Thus spake the seraph; and forthwith
Appeared a shining throng
Of angels, praising God, who thus
Addressed their joyful song:

6. "All glory be to God on high,
And to the earth be peace;
Good-will henceforth from Heaven to men
Begin, and never cease!"

164

1. My God, the spring of all my joys,
The life of my delights,
The glory of my brightest days,
And comfort of my nights!

2. In darkest shades if He appear,
My dawning is begun;
He is my soul's sweet morning star,
And He my rising sun.

3. The opening heavens around me shine
With beams of sacred bliss,
While Jesus shows His heart is mine,
And whispers, I am His.

4. My soul would leave this heavy clay,
At that transporting word;
Run up with joy the shining way,
To embrace my dearest Lord.

165

1. It came upon the midnight clear,
That glorious song of old,
From angels bending near the earth
To touch their harps of gold:

2. "Peace to the earth, good-will to man,
From heaven's all-gracious King:"
The earth in solemn stillness lay,
To hear the angels sing.

3. Still through the cloven skies they come,
With peaceful wings unfurled;
And still celestial music floats
O'er all the weary world.

4. Above its sad and lowly plains
They bend on heavenly wing,
And ever o'er its Babel sounds,
The blessèd angels sing.

5. For lo, the days are hastening on,
By prophet-bards foretold,
When with the ever-circling years
Comes round the age of gold,

6. When peace shall over all the earth
Its final splendors fling,
And the whole world send back the song
Which now the angels sing.

166

1. On Jordan's stormy banks I stand,
And cast a wishful eye
To Canaan's fair and happy land,
Where my possessions lie.

2. O the transporting, rapturous scene
That rises to my sight!
Sweet fields arrayed in living green,
And rivers of delight!

3. All o'er those wide extended plains
Shines one eternal day;
There God, the Son, forever reigns,
And scatters night away.

4. When shall I reach that happy place,
And be forever blest!
When shall I see my Father's face,
And in His bosom rest!

167

1 Jesus, the very thought of Thee
With sweetness fills the breast;
But sweeter far Thy face to see,
And in Thy presence rest.

2 Nor voice can sing, nor heart can frame,
Nor can the memory find
A sweeter sound than Thy blest name,
O Saviour of mankind!

3 O hope of every contrite heart!
O joy of all the meek!
To those who fall, how kind Thou art,
How good to those who seek!

4 But what to those who find? Ah! this
Nor tongue nor pen can show;
The love of Jesus, what it is,
None but His loved ones know.

5 Jesus, our only joy be Thou,
As Thou our prize wilt be;
Jesus, be Thou our glory now,
And through eternity!

168 Psalm 42.

1 As pants the hart for cooling streams,
When heated in the chase,
So longs my soul, O God, for Thee,
And Thy refreshing grace.

2 For Thee, my God, the living God,
My thirsty soul doth pine;
O when shall I behold Thy face,
Thou Majesty Divine!

3 Why restless, why cast down, my soul?
Trust God who will employ
His aid for thee, and change these sighs
To thankful hymns of joy.

4 I sigh to think of happier days,
When Thou, O Lord, wast nigh;
When every heart was tuned to praise,
And none more blest than I.

5 Why restless, why cast down, my soul?
Hope still, and thou shalt sing
The praise of Him who is thy God,
Thy health's eternal spring.

169

1 Jesus, these eyes have never seen
That radiant form of Thine;
The veil of sense hangs dark between
Thy blessèd face and mine.

2 I see Thee not, I hear Thee not,
Yet art Thou oft with me;
And earth hath ne'er so dear a spot,
As where I meet with Thee.

3 Like some bright dream that comes
    unsought
When slumbers o'er me roll,
Thine image ever fills my thought,
And charms my ravished soul.

4 Yet though I have not seen, and still
Must rest in faith alone,
I love Thee, dearest Lord, and will,
Unseen but not Unknown.

5 When death these mortal eyes shall seal
And still this throbbing heart,
The rending veil shall Thee reveal,
All glorious as Thou art!

170

1 Thou lovely Source of true delight
Whom I unseen adore,
Unveil Thy beauties to my sight,
That I may love Thee more.

2 Thy glory o'er creation shines;
But in Thy sacred word
I read in fairer, brighter lines,
My bleeding, dying Lord.

3 'Tis here, whene'er my comforts droop,
And sin and sorrow rise,
Thy love with cheerful beams of hope
My fainting breast supplies.

4 Jesus, my Lord, my life, my light,
O come with blissful ray;
Break radiant through the shades o.
    night,
And chase my fears away!

5 Then shall my soul with rapture trace
The wonders of Thy love;
But the full glories of Thy face
Are only known above.

171

1 How sweet the name of Jesus sounds
 In a believer's ear!
 It soothes his sorrows, heals his wounds,
 And drives away his fear.

2 It makes the wounded spirit whole,
 And calms the troubled breast;
 'Tis manna to the hungry soul,
 And to the weary rest.

3 By Thee, my prayers acceptance gain,
 Although with sin defiled;
 Satan accuses me in vain,
 And I am owned a child.

4 Weak is the effort of my heart,
 And cold my warmest thought;
 But when I see Thee as Thou art,
 I'll praise Thee as I ought.

5 Till then I would Thy love proclaim
 With every fleeting breath;
 And may the music of Thy name
 Refresh my soul in death.

172

1 The Saviour! O what endless charms
 Dwell in the blissful sound!
 Its influence every fear disarms,
 And spreads sweet comfort round.

2 The Almighty Former of the skies
 Stooped to our vile abode,
 While angels viewed with wandering eyes
 And hailed the incarnate God.

3 O the rich depths of love divine!
 Of bliss a boundless store!
 Dear Saviour, let me call Thee mine,
 I cannot wish for more!

4 On Thee alone my hope relies,
 Beneath Thy cross I fall;
 My Lord, my life, my sacrifice,
 My Saviour, and my all!

173

1 Majestic sweetness sits enthroned
 Upon the Saviour's brow;
 His head with radiant glories crowned,
 His lips with grace o'erflow.

2 To Him I owe my life and breath,
 And all the joys I have;
 He makes me triumph over death,
 He saves me from the grave.

3 To heaven, the place of His abode,
 He brings my weary feet,
 Shows me the glories of my God,
 And makes my joy complete.

4 Since from His bounty I receive
 Such proofs of love divine,
 Had I a thousand hearts to give,
 Lord, they should all be Thine.

174

1 With joy we meditate the grace
 Of our High-Priest above;
 His heart is made of tenderness,
 His bosom glows with love.

2 Touched with a sympathy within,
 He knows our feeble frame;
 He knows what sore temptations mean,
 For He hath felt the same.

3 He, in the days of feeble flesh,
 Poured out His cries and tears;
 And in His measure feels afresh
 What every member bears.

4 Then let our humble faith address
 His mercy and His power;
 We shall obtain delivering grace
 In the distressing hour.

175

1 God of the sunlight hours, how sad
 Would evening shadows be,
 Or night, in deeper sable clad,
 If aught were dark to Thee!

2 How mournfully that golden gleam
 Would touch the thoughtful heart,
 If, with its soft, retiring beam,
 We saw Thy love depart.

3 But though the gathering gloom may hide
 Those gentle rays awhile,
 Yet they who in Thy house abide
 Shall ever share Thy smile.

4 Then let creation's volume close,
 Though every page be bright;
 On Thine, still open, we repose
 With more intense delight.

176

1 There is an hour of peaceful rest
  To mourning wanderers given;
  There is a joy for souls distrest
  A balm for every wounded breast,—
  'Tis found above in heaven.

2 There is a home for weary souls,
  By sin and sorrow driven,
  When tossed on life's tempestuous shoals,
  Where storms arise and ocean rolls,
  And all is drear but heaven.

3 There fragrant flowers immortal bloom,
  And joys supreme are given;
  There rays divine disperse the gloom;
  Beyond the confines of the tomb
  Appears the dawn of heaven.

177

1 Come, Holy Spirit, heavenly Dove,
  With all Thy quickening powers,
  Kindle a flame of sacred love
  In these cold hearts of ours.

2 In vain we tune our formal songs,
  In vain we strive to rise;
  Hosannas languish on our tongues,
  And our devotion dies.

3 Dear Lord, and shall we ever live
  At this poor, dying rate!
  Our love so faint, so cold to Thee,
  And Thine to us so great!

4 Come, Holy Spirit, heavenly Dove,
  With all Thy quickening powers!
  Come, shed abroad a Saviour's love,
  And that shall kindle ours.

178

1 O for a closer walk with God,
  A calm and heavenly frame,
  A light to shine upon the road
  That leads me to the Lamb!

2 Return, O holy Dove, return,
  Sweet messenger of rest!
  I hate the sins that made Thee mourn,
  And drove Thee from my breast.

3 The dearest idol I have known,
  Whate'er that idol be,
  Help me to tear it from Thy throne,
  And worship only Thee.

4 So shall my walk be close with God,
  Calm and serene my frame;
  So purer light shall mark the road
  That leads me to the Lamb.

179

1 I love to steal awhile away
  From every cumbering care,
  And spend the hours of setting day
  In humble, grateful prayer.

2 I love, in solitude, to shed
  The penitential tear;
  And all His promises to plead
  Where none but God is near.

3 I love to think on mercies past,
  And future good implore;
  And all my cares and sorrows cast
  On Him whom I adore.

4 I love, by faith, to take a view
  Of brighter scenes in heaven;
  The prospect doth my strength renew,
  While here by tempests driven.

5 Thus, when life's toilsome day is o'er,
  May its departing ray
  Be calm as this impressive hour,
  And lead to endless day.

180

1 Prayer is the soul's sincere desire,
  Uttered or unexpressed;
  The motion of a hidden fire
  That trembles in the breast.

2 Prayer is the burden of a sigh,
  The falling of a tear,
  The upward glancing of an eye
  When none but God is near.

3 Prayer is the simplest form of speech
  That infant lips can try;
  Prayer the sublimest strains that reach
  The Majesty on high.

4 Prayer is the Christian's vital breath,
  The Christian's native air,
  His watchword at the gates of death;
  He enters heaven with prayer.

COWPER. C. M.

BURNAP. C. M.

TRENT. C. M.

181

1 There is a fountain filled with blood
  Drawn from Immanuel's veins;
  And sinners, plunged beneath that flood,
  Lose all their guilty stains.

2 The dying thief rejoiced to see
  That fountain in his day;
  And there may I, though vile as he,
  Wash all my sins away.

3 Dear dying Lamb! Thy precious blood
  Shall never lose its power,
  Till all the ransomed church of God
  Be saved, to sin no more.

4 E'er since, by faith, I saw the stream
  Thy flowing wounds supply,
  Redeeming love has been my theme,
  And shall be till I die.

5 Then in a nobler, sweeter song,
  I'll sing Thy power to save,
  When this poor lisping, stammering tongue
  Lies silent in the grave.

182 Psalm 23.

1 The Lord's my Shepherd, I'll not want;
  He makes me down to lie
  In pastures green; He leadeth me
  The quiet waters by.

2 My soul He doth restore again;
  And me to walk doth make
  Within the paths of righteousness,
  Even for His own Name's sake.

3 Yea, though I walk in death's dark vale,
  Yet will I fear none ill;
  For Thou art with me, and Thy rod
  And staff me comfort still.

4 My table Thou hast furnished
  In presence of my foes;
  My head Thou dost with oil anoint,
  And my cup overflows.

5 Goodness and mercy, all my life,
  Shall surely follow me;
  And in God's house for evermore
  My dwelling-place shall be.

183

1 And did the Holy and the Just,
  The Sovereign of the skies,
  Stoop down to wretchedness and dust,
  That guilty man might rise!

2 He took the dying sinner's place,
  And suffered in his stead;
  For man, O miracle of grace!
  For man the Saviour bled.

3 Dear Lord, what heavenly wonders dwell
  In Thine atoning blood!
  By this are sinners saved from hell,
  And rebels brought to God.

4 Jesus, my soul adoring, bends
  To love so full, so free;
  And may I hope that love extends
  Its sacred power to me!

5 What glad return can I impart
  For favors so divine?
  O take my all, this worthless heart,
  And make it only Thine!

184

1 See Israel's gentle Shepherd stand,
  With all-engaging charms;
  Hark! how He calls the tender lambs,
  And folds them in His arms.

2 "Permit them to approach," He cries,
  "Nor scorn their humble name;
  For 'twas to bless such souls as these
  The Lord of angels came."

3 We bring them, Lord, in thankful hands,
  And yield them up to Thee,
  Joyful that we ourselves are Thine—
  Thine let our offspring be.

185

1 "Forbid them not," the Saviour cried,
  "But suffer them to come;"
  Ah, then maternal tears were dried,
  And unbelief was dumb.

2 Lord, we believe, and we obey;
  We bring them at Thy word;
  Be Thou our children's strength and stay,
  Their portion and reward.

186

1 Amazing grace! how sweet the sound
  That saved a wretch like me!
  I once was lost, but now am found;
  Was blind, but now I see.

2 'Twas grace that taught my heart to fear,
  And grace my fears relieved;
  How precious did that grace appear
  The hour I first believed!

3 Through many dangers, toils, and snares,
  I have already come;
  'Tis grace has brought me safe thus far,
  And grace will lead me home.

4 The earth shall soon dissolve like snow,
  The sun forbear to shine;
  But God who called me here below,
  Will be forever mine.

187

1 Alas! and did my Saviour bleed,
  And did my Sovereign die!
  Would He devote that sacred head
  For such a worm as I!

2 Was it for crimes that I had done
  He groaned upon the tree!
  Amazing pity! grace unknown!
  And love beyond degree!

3 Well might the sun in darkness hide,
  And shut His glories in,
  When God, the mighty Maker, died
  For man, the creature's sin.

4 Thus might I hide my blushing face
  While His dear cross appears:
  Dissolve, my heart, in thankfulness!
  And melt, mine eyes, to tears!

5 But drops of grief can ne'er repay
  The debt of love I owe;
  Here, Lord, I give myself away,
  'Tis all that I can do.

188

1 If human kindness meets return,
  And owns the grateful tie;
  If tender thoughts within us burn
  To feel a friend is nigh:

2 O shall not warmer accents tell
  The gratitude we owe
  To Him who died our fears to quell,
  Our more than orphan's woe!

3 While yet His anguished soul surveyed
  Those pangs He would not flee,
  What love His latest words displayed:
  "Meet and remember me!"

4 Remember Thee! Thy death, Thy shame,
  Our sinful hearts to share!
  O memory, leave no other name
  But His recorded there!

189

1 Jesus, Thou art the sinner's Friend;
  As such I look to Thee;
  Now in the fulness of Thy love,
  O Lord, remember me.

2 Remember Thy pure word of grace,
  Remember Calvary;
  Remember all Thy dying groans,
  And then remember me.

3 Lord, I am guilty, I am vile,
  But Thy salvation's free;
  Then in Thine all-abounding grace,
  Dear Lord, remember me.

4 And, when I close my eyes in death,
  When creature-helps all flee,
  Then, O my dear Redeemer-God,
  I pray, remember me.

190

1 O Thou, whose tender mercy hears
  Contrition's humble sigh;
  Whose hand, indulgent, wipes the tears
  From sorrow's weeping eye;

2 See, low before Thy throne of grace,
  A wretched wanderer mourn;
  Hast Thou not bid me seek Thy face!
  Hast Thou not said, "Return"!

3 O shine on this benighted heart!
  With beams of mercy shine!
  And let Thy healing voice impart
  A taste of joys divine.

191

1 O could our thoughts and wishes fly
Above these gloomy shades,
To those bright worlds beyond the sky,
Which sorrow ne'er invades!

2 There joys unseen by mortal eyes,
Or reason's feeble ray,
In ever-blooming prospects rise,
Unconscious of decay.

3 Lord! send a beam of light divine,
To guide our upward aim!
With one reviving touch of Thine,
Our languid hearts inflame!

4 O then, on faith's sublimest wing,
Our ardent hope shall rise
To those bright scenes, where pleasures spring,
Immortal, in the skies.

192 Psalm 34.

1 Through all the changing scenes of life,
In trouble and in joy,
The praises of my God shall still
My heart and tongue employ.

2 The hosts of God encamp around
The dwellings of the just;
Deliverance He affords to all
Who on His succor trust.

3 O make but trial of His love!
Experience will decide
How blest are they, and only they,
Who in His truth confide.

4 Fear Him, ye saints, and you will then
Have nothing else to fear;
Make you His service your delight;
He'll make your wants His care.

193 Psalm 119.

1 O how I love Thy holy law!
'Tis daily my delight;
And thence my meditations draw
Divine advice by night.

2 My waking eyes prevent the day
To meditate Thy word;
My soul with longing melts away
To hear Thy gospel, Lord.

3 How doth Thy word my heart engage,
How well employ my tongue,
And in my tiresome pilgrimage
Yield me a heavenly song!

4 When nature sinks, and spirits droop,
Thy promises of grace
Are pillars to support my hope,
And there I write Thy praise.

194

1 O for a heart to praise my God,
A heart from sin set free,
A heart that always feels Thy blood,
So freely spilt for me!

2 A heart resigned, submissive, meek,
My great Redeemer's throne;
Where only Christ is heard to speak,
Where Jesus reigns alone!

3 A heart in every thought renewed,
And full of love divine;
Perfect, and right, and pure, and good,
A copy, Lord, of Thine!

4 Thy nature, gracious Lord, impart;
Come quickly from above;
Write Thy new name upon my heart,
Thy new, best name of Love.

195

1 How precious is the book divine,
By inspiration given!
Bright as a lamp its doctrines shine
To guide our souls to heaven.

2 O'er all the strait and narrow way
Its radiant beams are cast;
A light whose never-weary ray
Grows brightest at the last.

3 It sweetly cheers our drooping hearts,
In this dark vale of tears;
Life, light, and joy it still imparts,
And quells our rising fears.

4 This lamp through all the tedious night
Of life shall guide our way,
Till we behold the clearer light
Of an eternal day.

196

1 Father, whate'er of earthly bliss
Thy sovereign will denies,
Accepted at Thy throne of grace,
Let this petition rise:

2 Give me a calm, a thankful heart,
From every murmur free;
The blessings of Thy grace impart,
And let me live to Thee.

3 Let the sweet hope that Thou art mine
My life and death attend;
Thy presence through my journey shine,
And crown my journey's end.

197

1 Lord, when we bend before Thy throne
And our confessions pour.
Teach us to feel the sins we own,
And hate what we deplore.

2 Our broken spirit pitying see;
True penitence impart;
Then let a kindling glance from Thee
Beam hope upon the heart.

3 When we disclose our wants in prayer,
May we our wills resign;
And not a thought our bosoms share,
Which is not wholly Thine.

4 May faith each weak petition fill,
And waft it to the skies,
And teach our hearts 'tis goodness still
That grants it or denies.

198

1 Thou art the Way; to Thee alone
From sin and death we flee;
And he who would the Father seek,
Must seek Him, Lord, by Thee.

2 Thou art the Truth; Thy word alone
True wisdom can impart;
Thou only canst inform the mind
And purify the heart.

3 Thou art the Life; the rending tomb
Proclaims Thy conquering arm,
And those who put their trust in Thee
Nor death nor hell shall harm.

4 Thou art the Way, the Truth, the Life;
Grant us that Way to know,
That Truth to keep, that Life to win
Whose joys eternal flow.

199

1 Jesus, at whose supreme command,
We now approach to God,
Before us in Thy vesture stand,
Thy vesture dipped in blood.

2 Obedient to Thy gracious word,
We break the hallowed bread,
Commemorate our dying Lord,
And trust on Thee to feed.

3 The cup of blessing, blest by Thee,
Let it Thy blood impart;
The bread Thy mystic body be,
And cheer each languid heart.

4 Now, Saviour, now Thyself reveal,
And make Thy nature known;
Affix Thy blessèd Spirit's seal,
And stamp us for Thine own.

200

1 My God! my Father! blissful name!
O may I call thee mine!
May I with sweet assurance claim
A portion so divine!

2 This only can my fears control,
And bid my sorrows fly:
What harm can ever reach my soul
Beneath my Father's eye!

3 Whate'er Thy providence denies,
I calmly would resign;
For Thou art good, and just, and wise
O bend my will to Thine.

4 Whate'er Thy sacred will ordains,
O give me strength to bear;
Let me but know my Father reigns,
And trust His tender care.

5 My God! my Father! be Thy Name
My solace and my stay;
O wilt Thou seal my humble claim,
And drive my fears away.

201

1 I HEARD the voice of Jesus say,
"Come unto me and rest;
Lay down, thou weary one, lay down
Thy head upon my breast."

2 I came to Jesus as I was,
Weary, and worn, and sad;
I found in Him a resting-place,
And He has made me glad.

3 I heard the voice of Jesus say,
"Behold, I freely give
The living water; thirsty one,
Stoop down, and drink, and live."

4 I came to Jesus, and I drank
Of that life-giving stream;
My thirst was quenched, my soul revived,
And now I live in Him.

5 I heard the voice of Jesus say,
"I am this dark world's Light;
Look unto Me, thy morn shall rise,
And all Thy day be bright."

6 I looked to Jesus, and I found
In Him my star, my sun;
And in that light of life I'll walk
Till all my journey's done.

202

1 How sweet and awful is the place,
With Christ within the doors,
While everlasting love displays
The choicest of her stores!

2 While all our hearts, and all our songs,
Join to admire the feast,
Each of us cries with thankful tongue,
"Lord, why was I a guest?"

3 'Twas the same love that spread the feast,
That sweetly forced us in;
Else we had still refused to taste,
And perished in our sin.

4 Pity the nations, O our God!
Constrain the earth to come;
Send Thy victorious word abroad,
And bring the strangers home.

203

1 DEAR Refuge of my weary soul,
On Thee, when sorrows rise,
On Thee, when waves of trouble roll,
My fainting hope relies.

2 To Thee I tell each rising grief,
For Thou alone canst heal;
Thy word can bring a sweet relief
For every pain I feel.

3 But O when gloomy doubts prevail,
I fear to call Thee mine;
The springs of comfort seem to fail,
And all my hopes decline.

4 Yet, gracious God, where shall I flee!
Thou art my only trust;
And still my soul would cleave to Thee,
Though prostrate in the dust.

5 Thy mercy-seat is open still;
Here let my soul retreat,
With humble hope attend Thy will,
And wait beneath Thy feet.

204

1 THROUGH sorrow's night and danger's path,
Amid the deepening gloom,
We, soldiers of an injured King,
Are marching to the tomb.

2 There, when the turmoil is no more,
And all our powers decay,
Our cold remains in solitude
Shall sleep the years away.

3 Our labors done, securely laid
In this our last retreat,
Unheeded, o'er our silent dust,
The storms of life shall beat.

4 These ashes poor, this little dust,
Our Father's care shall keep,
Till the last angel rise and break
The long and dreary sleep.

5 Then love's soft dew o'er every eye
Shall shed its mildest rays,
And the long silent dust shall burst
With shouts of endless praise.

205

1 Why do we mourn departing friends,
 Or shake at death's alarms?
 'Tis but the voice that Jesus sends,
 To call them to His arms.

2 Are we not tending upward too,
 As fast as time can move!
 Nor should we wish the hours more slow,
 To keep us from our Love.

3 The graves of all the saints He blessed,
 And softened every bed:
 Where should the dying members rest
 But with their dying Head!

4 Thence He arose, ascending high,
 And showed our feet the way;
 Up to the Lord our flesh shall fly,
 At the great rising-day.

5 Then let the last loud trumpet sound,
 And bid our kindred rise:
 Awake, ye nations under ground;
 Ye saints, ascend the skies.

206

1 Plunged in a gulf of dark despair
 We wretched sinners lay,
 Without one cheerful beam of hope,
 Or spark of glimmering day.

2 With pitying eyes the Prince of grace
 Beheld our helpless grief;
 He saw, and—O amazing love!—
 He ran to our relief.

3 Down from the shining seats above
 With joyful haste He fled,
 Entered the grave in mortal flesh,
 And dwelt among the dead.

4 O for this love let rocks and hills
 Their lasting silence break;
 And all harmonious human tongues
 The Saviour's praises speak.

5 Angels, assist our mighty joys;
 Strike all your harps of gold;
 But when you raise your highest notes,
 His love can ne'er be told.

207

1 Why should our tears in sorrow flow
 When God recalls His own,
 And bids them leave a world of woe,
 For an immortal crown!

2 Is not e'en death a gain to those
 Whose life to God was given!
 Gladly to earth their eyes they close,
 To open them in heaven.

3 Their toils are past, their work is done,
 And they are fully blest;
 They fought the fight, the victory won,
 And entered into rest.

4 Then let our sorrows cease to flow,
 God has recalled His own;
 And let our hearts, in every woe,
 Still say, "Thy will be done!"

208

1 Must Jesus bear the cross alone,
 And all the world go free?
 No; there's a cross for every one,
 And there's a cross for me.

2 The consecrated cross I'll bear,
 Till death shall set me free;
 And then go home my crown to wear,
 For there's a crown for me.

3 How happy are the saints above,
 Who once went sorrowing here!
 But now they taste unmingled love,
 And joy without a tear.

4 Upon the crystal pavement, down
 At Jesus' piercèd feet,
 Joyful I'll cast my golden crown,
 And His dear name repeat.

5 And palms shall wave, and harps shall ring,
 Beneath heaven's arches high;
 The Lord that lives, the ransomed sing,
 That lives, no more to die.

6 O precious cross! O glorious crown!
 O resurrection day!
 Ye angels, from the stars flash down,
 And bear my soul away.

209

1 While Thee I seek, protecting Power,
Be my vain wishes stilled;
And may this consecrated hour
With better hopes be filled!
Thy love the power of thought bestowed;
To Thee my thoughts would soar;
Thy mercy o'er my life has flowed;
That mercy I adore.

2 In each event of life, how clear
Thy ruling hand I see!
Each blessing to my soul more dear
Because conferred by Thee.
In every joy that crowns my days,
In every pain I bear,
My heart shall find delight in praise,
Or seek relief in prayer.

3 When gladness wings my favored hour,
Thy love my thoughts shall fill;
Resigned when storms of sorrow lower,
My soul shall meet Thy will.
My lifted eye, without a tear,
The gathering storm shall see;
My steadfast heart shall know no fear,
That heart shall rest on Thee.

210
Psalm 63.

1 Early, my God, without delay,
I haste to seek Thy face;
My thirsty spirit faints away
Without Thy cheering grace.

2 So pilgrims on the scorching sand,
Beneath a burning sky,
Long for a cooling stream at hand,
And they must drink or die.

3 I've seen Thy glory and Thy power
Through all Thy temple shine;
My God, repeat that heavenly hour,
That vision so divine!

4 Not life itself, with all its joys,
Can my best passions move;
Or raise so high my cheerful voice,
As Thy forgiving love.

5 Thus, till my last expiring day,
I'll bless my God and King;
Thus will I lift my hands to pray,
And tune my lips to sing.

211

1 When all Thy mercies, O my God,
My rising soul surveys,
Transported with the view, I'm lost
In wonder, love, and praise.
Ten thousand thousand precious gifts
My daily thanks employ;
Nor is the least a cheerful heart
That tastes those gifts with joy.

2 Through every period of my life
Thy goodness I'll pursue;
And after death, in distant worlds,
The glorious theme renew.
Through all eternity, to Thee
A joyful song I'll raise;
But O eternity's too short
To utter all Thy praise!

212

1 How sweet, how heavenly is the sight,
When those who love the Lord
In one another's peace delight,
And so fulfil His word.

2 When each can feel his brother's sigh,
And with him bear a part;
When sorrow flows from eye to eye,
And joy from heart to heart!

3 When, free from envy, scorn, and pride,
Our wishes all above,
Each can his brother's failings hide,
And show a brother's love!

4 Let love, in one delightful stream,
Through every bosom flow;
And union sweet, and dear esteem,
In every action glow.

5 Love is the golden chain that binds
The happy souls above;
And he's an heir of heaven who finds
His bosom glow with love.

213

1 Lo, on a narrow neck of land,
'Twixt two unbounded seas I stand,
Yet how insensible!
A point of time, a moment's space,
Removes me to yon heavenly place,
Or shuts me up in hell.

2 O God, my inmost soul convert,
And deeply on my thoughtful heart
Eternal things impress;
Give me to feel their solemn weight,
And save me ere it be too late;
Wake me to righteousness.

3 Before me place, in bright array,
The pomp of that tremendous day,
When Thou with clouds shall come
To judge the nations at Thy bar;
And tell me, Lord, shall I be there,
To meet a joyful doom?

4 Then, Saviour, then my soul receive,
Transported from this vale, to live
And reign with Thee above;
Where faith is sweetly lost in sight,
And hope in full, supreme delight,
And everlasting love.

214

1 O Thou, who hear'st the prayer of faith,
Wilt Thou not save a soul from death,
That casts itself on Thee?
I have no refuge of my own,
But fly to what my Lord hath done,
And suffered once for me.

2 Slain in the guilty sinner's stead,
His spotless righteousness I plead
And His availing blood;
Thy merit, Lord my robe shall be;
Thy merit shall atone for me,
And bring me near to God.

3 Then save me from eternal death,
The Spirit of adoption breathe,
His consolations send;
By Him some word of life impart,
And sweetly whisper to my heart,
"Thy Maker is thy Friend."

215

1 When Thou, my righteous Judge, shalt come
To take Thy ransomed people home,
Shall I among them stand?
Shall such a worthless worm as I,
Who sometimes am afraid to die,
Be found at Thy right hand?

2 I love to meet Thy people now,
Before Thy feet with them to bow,
Though vilest of them all;
But—can I bear the piercing thought—
What if my name should be left out,
When Thou for them shalt call!

3 Among Thy saints let me be found,
Whene'er the Archangel's trump shall
To see Thy smiling face;   [sound,
Then loudest of the throng I'll sing,
While heaven's resounding mansions ring
With shouts of sovereign grace.

216

1 When, Lord, to this our western land,
Led by Thy providential hand,
Our wandering fathers came,
Their ancient homes, their friends in youth,
Sent forth the heralds of Thy truth
To keep them in Thy name.

2 Then, through our solitary coast,
The desert features soon were lost;
Thy temples there arose;
Our shores, as culture made them fair,
Were hallowed by Thy rites, by prayer,
And blossomed as the rose.

3 And O may we repay this debt
To regions solitary yet,
Within our spreading land;
There brethren from our common home,
Still westward, like our fathers, roam;
Still guided by Thy hand.

4 Saviour, we own this debt of love;
O shed Thy Spirit from above,
To move each Christian breast;
Till heralds shall Thy truth proclaim,
And temples rise to fix Thy name,
Through all our desert west.

217

1 O COULD I speak the matchless worth,
O could I sound the glories forth,
Which in my Saviour shine,
I'd soar and touch the heavenly strings,
And vie with Gabriel while he sings
In notes almost divine.

2 I'd sing the precious blood He spilt,
My ransom from the dreadful guilt
Of sin and wrath divine;
I'd sing His glorious righteousness,
In which all-perfect heavenly dress
My soul shall ever shine.

3 I'd sing the characters He bears,
And all the forms of love He wears,
Exalted on His throne;
In loftiest songs of sweetest praise,
I would to everlasting days
Make all His glories known.

4 Well, the delightful day will come
When my dear Lord will bring me home,
And I shall see His face;
Then with my Saviour, Brother, Friend,
A blest eternity I'll spend,
Triumphant in His grace.

218

1 O LOVE divine, how sweet thou art!
When shall I find my willing heart
All taken up by thee?
I thirst, I faint, I die to prove
The greatness of redeeming love,
The love of Christ to me.

2 God only knows the love of God;
O that it now were shed abroad
In this poor, stony heart!
For love I sigh, for love I pine;
This only portion, Lord, be mine,
Be mine this better part.

3 O that I could forever sit
With Mary at my Saviour's feet!
Be this my happy choice;
My only care, delight, and bliss,
My joy, my heaven on earth, be this,
To hear the Bridegroom's voice.

219

1 MY God, Thy boundless love I praise;
How bright on high its glories blaze!
How sweetly bloom below!
It streams from Thy eternal throne;
Through heaven its joys forever run,
And o'er the earth they flow.

2 But in Thy word, I see it shine
With grace and glories more divine,
Proclaiming sin forgiven;
There Faith, bright cherub, points the way
To realms of everlasting day,
And opens all her heaven.

3 Then let the love that makes me blest
With cheerful praise inspire my breast,
And ardent gratitude;
And all my thoughts and passions tend
To Thee, my Father and my Friend,
My soul's eternal good.

220

1 JESUS, enthroned and glorified
At Thy Almighty Father's side,
Thy people's prayer inspire!
Thou art alive for evermore;
O then on us Thy Spirit pour;
Baptize us now with fire.

2 Thou hast received rich gifts for men;
Now let the Holy Ghost again
On all Thy Church descend;
Give boldness, power, and tongues of flame
To all who name Thy blessed name;
Uphold them and defend.

3 The fulness of Thy life bestow
On us Thy members here below;
Revive each fainting heart;
Each sick and wounded spirit heal,
Thy beauty to our souls reveal,
Thy light and love impart.

4 Blest Comforter, celestial dove,
Thou Lord of life, Thou fount of love,
Be Thou our inward guest;
Illumed and sanctified by Thee,
Thy living temples let us be,
Thine everlasting rest.

221

1 STAND up, and bless the Lord,
   Ye people of His choice;
   Stand up, and bless the Lord your God,
   With heart, and soul, and voice.

2 O for a living flame,
   From His own altar brought,
   To touch our lips, our minds inspire,
   And wing to heaven our thought!

3 God is our strength and song,
   And His salvation ours;
   Then be His love in Christ proclaimed,
   With all our ransomed powers.

4 Stand up, and bless the Lord,
   The Lord your God adore;
   Stand up, and bless His glorious Name
   Henceforth for evermore.

222

1 AWAKE, and sing the song
   Of Moses and the Lamb;
   Tune every heart and every tongue
   To praise the Saviour's name.

2 Sing of His dying love;
   Sing of His rising power;
   Sing how He intercedes above
   For those whose sins He bore.

3 Sing on your heavenly way,
   Ye ransomed sinners, sing!
   Sing on, rejoicing every day
   In Christ, the eternal King.

4 Soon shall we hear Him say,
   "Ye blessed children, come!"
   Soon will He call us hence away,
   To our eternal home.

5 Soon shall our raptured tongue
   His endless praise proclaim;
   And sweeter voices tune the song
   Of Moses and the Lamb.

223

1 SOLDIERS of Christ, arise,
   And put your armor on,
   Strong in the strength which God supplies
   Through His eternal Son.

2 Strong in the Lord of hosts
   And in His mighty power,
   Who in the strength of Jesus trusts,
   Is more than conqueror.

3 Stand then in His great might,
   With all His strength endued,
   And take, to arm you for the fight,
   The panoply of God.

4 From strength to strength go on;
   Wrestle, and fight, and pray;
   Tread all the powers of darkness down,
   And win the well-fought day.

5 Still let the Spirit cry
   In all His soldiers, "Come!"
   Till Christ the Lord descends from high,
   And takes the conqueror home.

224

1 MY soul, be on thy guard!
   Ten thousand foes arise,
   And hosts of sin are pressing hard
   To draw thee from the skies.

2 O watch, and fight, and pray;
   The battle ne'er give o'er;
   Renew it boldly every day,
   And help divine implore.

3 Ne'er think the victory won,
   Nor lay thine armor down;
   Thy arduous work will not be done
   Till thou obtain thy crown.

4 Fight on, my soul, till death
   Shall bring thee to thy God!
   He'll take thee at thy parting breath
   Up to His blest abode.

225   Psalm 117.

1 THY name, Almighty Lord,
   Shall sound through distant lands;
   Great is Thy grace and sure Thy word;
   Thy truth forever stands.

2 Far be Thine honor spread,
   And long Thy praise endure,
   Till morning light and evening shade
   Shall be exchanged no more.

226

1 Raise your triumphant songs
   To an immortal tune;
   Let the wide earth resound the deeds
   Celestial grace has done.

2 Sing how Eternal Love
   Its chief Belovéd chose,
   And bade Him raise our wretched race
   From their abyss of woes.

3 His hand no thunder bears,
   No terror clothes His brow,
   No bolts to drive our guilty souls
   To fiercer flames below.

4 'Twas mercy filled the throne,
   And wrath stood silent by,
   When Christ was sent with pardons down
   To rebels doomed to die.

227   Psalm 95.

1 Come, sound His praise abroad,
   And hymns of glory sing!
   Jehovah is the sovereign God,
   The universal King.

2 He formed the deeps unknown;
   He gave the seas their bound;
   The watery worlds are all His own,
   And all the solid ground.

3 Come, worship at His throne,
   Come, bow before the Lord;
   We are His work, and not our own;
   He formed us by His word.

4 To-day attend His voice,
   Nor dare provoke His rod;
   Come, like the people of His choice,
   And own your gracious God.

228   Psalm 48.

1 Great is the Lord our God,
   And let His praise be great;
   He makes His churches His abode,
   His most delightful seat.

2 These temples of His grace,
   How beautiful they stand!
   The honors of our native place,
   And bulwarks of our land.

3 In Zion God is known,
   A refuge in distress;
   How bright hath His salvation shone
   Through all her palaces!

4 In every new distress
   We'll to His house repair;
   We'll think upon His wondrous grace,
   And seek deliverance there.

229

1 Come, we that love the Lord!
   And let our joys be known;
   Join in a song of sweet accord,
   And thus surround the throne.

2 Let those refuse to sing
   Who never knew our God;
   But children of the heavenly King
   May speak their joys abroad.

3 The hill of Zion yields
   A thousand sacred sweets,
   Before we reach the heavenly fields,
   Or walk the golden streets.

4 Then let our songs abound,
   And every tear be dry;
   We're marching through Immanuel's ground
   To fairer worlds on high.

230   Psalm 99.

1 The Lord Jehovah reigns;
   Let all the nations fear;
   Let sinners tremble at His throne,
   And saints be humble there.

2 Jesus the Saviour reigns;
   Let earth adore its Lord;
   Bright cherubs His attendants stand,
   And swift fulfil His word.

3 In Zion is His throne;
   His honors are divine;
   His church shall make His wonders known,
   For there His glories shine.

4 How holy is His Name!
   How terrible His praise!
   Justice, and truth, and judgment join
   In all His works of grace.

231

1 How beauteous are their feet
   Who stand on Zion's hill,
   Who bring salvation on their tongues,
   And words of peace reveal!

2 How charming is their voice!
   How sweet the tidings are!—
   "Zion, behold thy Saviour-King,
   He reigns and triumphs here!"

3 How happy are our ears
   That hear this joyful sound,
   Which kings and prophets waited for,
   And sought, but never found.

4 The watchmen join their voice,
   And tuneful notes employ;
   Jerusalem breaks forth in songs,
   And deserts learn the joy.

5 The Lord makes bare His arm,
   Through all the earth abroad;
   Let every nation now behold
   Their Saviour and their God.

232

1 WELCOME, sweet day of rest,
   That saw the Lord arise!
   Welcome to this reviving breast,
   And these rejoicing eyes!

2 The King Himself comes near,
   And feasts His saints to-day;
   Here may we sit and see Him here,
   And love, and praise, and pray.

3 One day amidst the place
   Where my dear God hath been,
   Is sweeter than ten thousand days
   Of pleasurable sin.

4 My willing soul would stay
   In such a frame as this,
   And sit and sing herself away
   To everlasting bliss.

233

1 GRACE! 'tis a charming sound,
   Harmonious to the ear!
   Heaven with the echo shall resound,
   And all the earth shall hear.

2 Grace first contrived the way
   To save rebellious man;
   And all the steps that grace display
   Which drew the wondrous plan.

3 Grace led my roving feet
   To tread the heavenly road;
   And new supplies each hour I meet,
   While pressing on to God.

4 Grace all the work shall crown,
   Through everlasting days;
   It lays in heaven the topmost stone,
   And well deserves the praise.

234

1 How charming is the place
   Where my Redeemer-God
   Unveils the beauties of His face,
   And sheds His love abroad!

2 Here on the mercy-seat,
   With radiant glory crowned,
   Our joyful eyes behold Him sit
   And smile on all around.

3 To Him our prayers and cries,
   Our humble souls present;
   He listens to our broken sighs,
   And grants us every want.

4 Give me, O Lord, a place
   Within Thy blest abode,
   Among the children of Thy grace,
   The servants of my God.

235   Psalm 103.

1 O BLESS the Lord, my soul!
   Let all within me join,
   And aid my tongue to bless His Name
   Whose favors are divine.

2 O bless the Lord, my soul!
   Nor let His mercies lie
   Forgotten in unthankfulness
   And without praises die.

3 He crowns thy life with love
   When ransomed from the grave;
   He who redeemed my soul from hell
   Hath sovereign power to save.

4 His wondrous works and ways
   He made by Moses known;
   But sent the world His truth and grace
   By His belovéd Son.

236

1 Sweet is the work, O Lord,
   Thy glorious acts to sing,
   To praise Thy Name and hear Thy word,
   And grateful offerings bring.

2 Sweet at the dawning light
   Thy boundless love to tell;
   And when approach the shades of night,
   Still on the theme to dwell.

3 Sweet on this day of rest
   To join, in heart and voice,
   With those who love and serve Thee best
   And in Thy name rejoice.

4 To songs of praise and joy
   Be every Sabbath given,
   That such may be our blest employ
   Eternally in heaven.

237 Psalm 19.

1 Behold the morning sun
   Begins his glorious way;
   His beams through all the nations run,
   And life and light convey.

2 But where the Gospel comes
   It spreads diviner light;
   It calls dead sinners from their tombs,
   And gives the blind their sight.

3 How perfect is Thy word,
   And all Thy judgments just;
   Forever sure Thy promise, Lord
   And men securely trust.

4 My gracious God, how plain
   Are Thy directions given!
   O may I never read in vain,
   But find the path to heaven.

238

1 To God the only wise,
   Our Saviour and our King,
   Let all the saints below the skies
   Their humble praises bring.

2 Tis His almighty love,
   His counsel and His care,
   Preserves us safe from sin and death,
   And every hurtful snare.

3 He will present our souls,
   Unblemished and complete,
   Before the glory of His face,
   With joys divinely great.

4 To our Redeemer-God
   Wisdom and power belong,
   Immortal crowns of majesty,
   And everlasting song.

239 Psalm 48.

1 Far as Thy name is known
   The world declares Thy praise;
   Thy saints, O Lord, before Thy throne
   Their songs of honor raise.

2 Let strangers walk around
   The city where we dwell,
   Compass and view the holy ground,
   And mark the building well,

3 The order of Thy house,
   The worship of Thy court,
   The cheerful songs, the solemn vows,
   And make a fair report.

4 How decent and how wise!
   How glorious to behold!
   Beyond the pomp that charms the eyes,
   And rites adorned with gold.

5 The God we worship now
   Will guide us till we die;
   Will be our God while here below,
   And ours above the sky.

240

1 We lift our hearts to Thee,
   Thou Day-star from on high;
   The sun itself is but Thy shade,
   Yet cheers both earth and sky.

2 O let Thy rising beams
   Dispel the shades of night;
   And let the glories of Thy love
   Come like the morning light!

3 How beauteous nature now!
   How dark and sad before!
   With joy we view the pleasing change,
   And nature's God adore.

4 May we this life improve
   To mourn for errors past;
   And live this short, revolving day
   As if it were our last.

241

1 Dear Saviour, we are Thine,
    By everlasting bands;
    Our names, our hearts, we would resign,
    Our souls, into Thy hands.

2 To Thee we still would cleave
    With ever-growing zeal;
    If millions tempt us Christ to leave,
    O let them ne'er prevail!

3 Thy Spirit shall unite
    Our souls to Thee, our Head;
    Shall form us to Thine image bright,
    That we Thy paths may tread.

4 Death may our souls divide
    From these abodes of clay;
    But love shall keep us near Thy side,
    Through all the gloomy way.

5 Since Christ and we are one,
    Why should we doubt or fear?
    If He in heaven has fixed His throne,
    He'll fix His members there.

242

1 Blest be the tie that binds
    Our hearts in Christian love;
    The fellowship of kindred minds
    Is like to that above.

2 Before our Father's throne,
    We pour our ardent prayers;
    Our fears, our hopes, our aims are one—
    Our comforts and our cares.

3 We share our mutual woes,
    Our mutual burdens bear;
    And often, for each other, flows
    The sympathizing tear.

4 When we asunder part,
    It gives us inward pain;
    But we shall still be joined in heart,
    And hope to meet again.

5 This glorious hope revives
    Our courage by the way;
    While each in expectation lives,
    And longs to see the day.

6 From sorrow, toil, and pain,
    And sin, we shall be free;
    And perfect love and friendship reign
    Through all eternity.

243

1 Blest be Thy love, dear Lord,
    That taught us this sweet way,
    Only to love Thee for Thyself,
    And for that love obey.

2 O Thou, our souls' chief hope,
    We to Thy mercy fly;
    Where'er we are, Thou canst protect;
    Whate'er we need, supply.

3 Whether we sleep or wake,
    To Thee we both resign;
    By night we see, as well as day,
    If Thy light on us shine.

4 Whether we live or die,
    Both we submit to Thee;
    In death we live, as well as life,
    If Thine in death we be.

244

1 Jesus, I live to Thee,
    The loveliest and best;
    My life in Thee, Thy life in me,
    In Thy blest love I rest.

2 Jesus, I die to Thee,
    Whenever death shall come;
    To die in Thee is life to me
    In my eternal home.

3 Whether to live or die,
    I know not which is best;
    To live in Thee is bliss to me,
    To die is endless rest.

4 Living or dying, Lord,
    I ask but to be Thine;
    My life in Thee, Thy life in me,
    Makes heaven forever mine.

245

1 O WHAT, if we are Christ's,
  Is earthly shame or loss?
  Bright shall the crown of glory be,
  When we have borne the cross.

2 Keen was the trial once,
  Bitter the cup of woe,
  When martyred saints, baptized in blood,
  Christ's sufferings shared below.

3 Bright is their glory now,
  Boundless their joy above,
  Where, on the bosom of their God,
  They rest in perfect love.

4 Lord, may that grace be ours,
  Like them in faith to bear
  All that of sorrow, grief, or pain
  May be our portion here!

246

1 FOREVER with the Lord!
  Amen! so let it be!
  Life from the dead is in that word,
  'Tis immortality.

2 Here in the body pent,
  Absent from Him I roam,
  Yet nightly pitch my moving tent
  A day's march nearer home.

3 My Father's house on high,
  Home of my soul, how near,
  At times, to faith's foreseeing eye,
  Thy golden gates appear!

4 Ah! then my spirit faints
  To reach the land I love,
  The bright inheritance of saints,
  Jerusalem above!

247

1 IT is not death to die,
  To leave this weary road,
  And, 'midst the brotherhood on high,
  To be at home with God.

2 It is not death to close
  The eye long dimmed by tears,
  And wake in glorious repose
  To spend eternal years.

3 It is not death to bear
  The wrench that sets us free
  From dungeon chain, to breathe the air
  Of boundless liberty.

4 It is not death to fling
  Aside this sinful dust,
  And rise on strong, exulting wing
  To live among the just.

5 Jesus, Thou Prince of Life,
  Thy chosen cannot die;
  Like Thee, they conquer in the strife,
  To reign with Thee on high.

248

1 COMMIT thou all thy griefs
  And ways into His hands,
  To His sure trust and tender care
  Who earth and heaven commands.

2 Through waves and clouds and storms
  He gently clears thy way;
  Wait thou His time, so shall this night
  Soon end in joyous day.

3 What though thou rulest not,
  Yet heaven and earth and hell
  Proclaim, God sitteth on the throne,
  And ruleth all things well!

4 Far, far above thy thought
  His counsel shall appear,
  When fully He the work hath wrought
  That caused thy needless fear.

5 Give to the winds thy fears;
  Hope, and be undismayed;
  God hears thy sighs and counts thy tears;
  God shall lift up thy head.

249
Psalm 137.

1 I love Thy kingdom, Lord,
The house of Thine abode,
The church our blest Redeemer saved
With His own precious blood.

2 I love Thy church, O God,
Her walls before Thee stand,
Dear as the apple of Thine eye,
And graven on Thy hand.

3 If e'er my heart forget
Her welfare or her woe,
Let every joy this heart forsake,
And every grief o'erflow.

4 For her my tears shall fall,
For her my prayers ascend;
To her my cares and toils be given
Till toils and care shall end.

5 Sure as Thy truth shall last,
To Zion shall be given
The brightest glories earth can yield,
And brighter bliss of heaven.

250

1 Not all the blood of beasts
On Jewish altars slain,
Could give the guilty conscience peace,
Or wash away the stain.

2 But Christ, the heavenly Lamb,
Takes all our sins away;
A sacrifice of nobler name
And richer blood than they.

3 My faith would lay her hand
On that dear head of Thine,
While like a penitent I stand,
And there confess my sin.

4 Believing, we rejoice
To see the curse remove;
We bless the Lamb with cheerful voice,
And sing His bleeding love.

251

1 A charge to keep I have;
A God to glorify,
A never-dying soul to save,
And fit it for the sky;

2 To serve the present age,
My calling to fulfil;
O may it all my powers engage
To do my Master's will!

3 Arm me with jealous care,
As in Thy sight to live;
And O Thy servant, Lord, prepare
A strict account to give.

4 Help me to watch and pray,
And on Thyself rely,
Assured, if I my trust betray,
I shall forever die.

252
Psalm 63.

1 My God, permit my tongue
This joy, to call Thee mine;
And let my early cries prevail
To taste Thy love divine.

2 My thirsty, fainting soul
Thy mercy does implore;
Not travellers in desert lands
Can pant for water more.

3 Within Thy churches, Lord,
I long to find my place,
Thy power and glory to behold,
And feel Thy quickening grace.

4 Since Thou hast been my help,
To Thee my spirit flies;
And on Thy watchful providence
My cheerful hope relies.

5 The shadow of Thy wings
My soul in safety keeps;
I follow where my Father leads,
And He supports my steps.

253

1 Blest are the sons of peace,
Whose hearts and hopes are one;
Whose kind designs to serve and please
Through all their actions run.

2 Blest is the pious house,
Where zeal and friendship meet;
Their songs of praise, their mingling vows,
Make their communion sweet.

3 Thus, on the heavenly hills,
The saints are blest above,
Where joy, like morning-dew, distils,
And all the air is love.

254

1 Come, Holy Spirit, come!
Let Thy bright beams arise,
Dispel the sorrow from our minds,
The darkness from our eyes.

2 Revive our drooping faith,
Our doubts and fears remove,
And kindle in our breasts the flame
Of never-dying love.

3 Convince us of our sin,
Then lead to Jesus' blood,
And to our wondering view reveal
The secret love of God.

4 'Tis Thine to cleanse the heart,
To sanctify the soul,
To pour fresh life in every part,
And new-create the whole.

255 Psalm 55.

1 How gentle God's commands,
How kind His precepts are!
Come, cast your burdens on the Lord,
And trust His constant care.

2 Beneath His watchful eye
His saints securely dwell;
That hand which bears creation up
Shall guide His children well.

3 Why should this anxious load
Press down your weary mind?
Haste to your Heavenly Father's throne,
And sweet refreshment find.

4 His goodness stands approved
Down to the present day;
I'll drop my burden at His feet,
And bear a song away.

256 Psalm 61.

1 When, overwhelmed with grief,
My heart within me dies;
Helpless, and far from all relief,
To heaven I lift mine eyes.

2 O lead me to the rock,
That's high above my head;
And make the covert of Thy wings
My shelter and my shade.

3 Within Thy presence, Lord,
Forever I'll abide;
Thou art the tower of my defence,
The refuge where I hide.

257

1 Blest Comforter Divine,
Let rays of heavenly love
Amid our gloom and darkness shine,
And guide our souls above.

2 Draw with Thy still small voice
From every sinful way,
And bid the mourning saint rejoice,
Though earthly joys decay.

3 By Thine inspiring breath
Make every cloud of care,
And e'en the gloomy vale of death,
A smile of glory wear.

4 O fill Thou every heart
With love to all our race;
Great Comforter, to us impart
These blessings of Thy grace.

258 Psalm 23.

1 The Lord my Shepherd is,
I shall be well supplied;
Since He is mine and I am His,
What can I want beside!

2 He leads me to the place
Where heavenly pasture grows,
Where living waters gently pass,
And full salvation flows.

3 If e'er I go astray,
He doth my soul reclaim;
And guides me in His own right way,
For His most holy name.

4 While He affords His aid,
I cannot yield to fear;
Though I should walk through death's dark shade,
My Shepherd's with me there.

5 Amid surrounding foes,
Thou dost my table spread;
My cup with blessings overflows,
And joy exalts my head.

259

1 O WHERE shall rest be found,
 Rest for the weary soul?
'Twere vain the ocean depths to sound,
 Or pierce to either pole.

2 The world can never give
 The bliss for which we sigh;
'Tis not the whole of life to live,
 Nor all of death to die.

3 Beyond this vale of tears
 There is a life above
Unmeasured by the flight of years;
 And all that life is love.

4 There is a death whose pang
 Outlasts the fleeting breath;
O what eternal horrors hang
 Around the second death!

5 Lord God of truth and grace,
 Teach us that death to shun!
Lest we be banished from Thy face,
 And evermore undone.

260

1 THE day is past and gone
 The evening shades appear;
O may I ever keep in mind
 The night of death draws near.

2 I lay my garments by,
 Upon my bed to rest;
So death shall soon disrobe us all,
 And leave my soul undrest.

3 Lord, keep me safe this night,
 Secure from all my fears;
May angels guard me while I sleep,
 Till morning light appears.

4 And when I early rise
 To view the unwearied sun,
May I set out to win the prize,
 And after glory run.

5 And when my days are past,
 And I from time remove,
O may I in Thy bosom rest,
 The bosom of Thy love.

261

1 JESUS invites His saints
 To meet around His board;
Here pardoned rebels sit and hold
 Communion with their Lord.

2 This holy bread and wine
 Maintain our fainting breath,
By union with our living Lord,
 And interest in His death.

3 Our heavenly Father calls
 Christ and His members one;
We, the young children of His love,
 And He, the First-born Son.

262

1 A PARTING hymn we sing
 Around Thy table, Lord;
Again our grateful tribute bring,
 Our solemn vows record.

2 Here have we seen Thy face,
 And felt Thy presence here;
So may the savor of Thy grace
 In word and life appear.

3 The purchase of Thy blood,
 By sin no longer led,
The path our dear Redeemer trod,
 May we rejoicing tread.

4 In self-forgetting love
 Be our communion shown,
Until we join the church above,
 And know as we are known.

263

1 THE Saviour kindly calls
 Our children to His breast;
He folds them in His gracious arms,
 Himself declares them blest.

2 "Let them approach," He cries,
 "Nor scorn their humble claim;
The heirs of heaven are such as these,
 For such as these I came."

3 With joy we bring them, Lord,
 Devoting them to Thee,
Imploring that as we are Thine,
 Thine may our offspring be.

264

1 Your harps, ye trembling saints,
Down from the willows take;
Loud to the praise of love divine
Bid every string awake.

2 Though in a foreign land,
We are not far from home;
And nearer to our house above
We every moment come.

3 His grace will to the end
Stronger and brighter shine;
Nor present things, nor things to come,
Shall quench the spark divine.

4 Soon shall our doubts and fears
Subside at His control;
His loving-kindness shall break through
The midnight of the soul.

265 [Hancock Street.]

1 For all Thy saints, O Lord,
Who strove in Thee to live,
Who followed Thee, obeyed, adored,
Our grateful hymn receive.

2 For all Thy saints, O Lord,
Accept our thankful cry,
Who counted Thee their great reward,
And strove in Thee to die.

3 They all, in life or death,
With Thee, their Lord in view,
Learned from Thy Holy Spirit's breath
To suffer and to do.

4 For this Thy Name we bless,
And humbly pray that we
May follow them in holiness,
And live and die in Thee.

266 [Middletown.]

1 Servant of God, well done!
Rest from thy loved employ;
The battle fought, the victory won,
Enter thy Master's joy!

2 The voice at midnight came;
He started up to hear;
A mortal arrow pierced his frame;
He fell, but felt no fear.

3 The pains of death are past,
Labor and sorrow cease,
And, life's long warfare closed at last,
His soul is found in peace.

4 Soldier of Christ, well done!
Praise be thy new employ;
And, while eternal ages run,
Rest in thy Saviour's joy!

267 [Middletown.]

1 Jesus my Shepherd is;
'Twas He that loved my soul,
'Twas He that washed me in His blood,
'Twas He that made me whole.

2 'Twas He that sought the lost,
That found the wandering sheep;
'Twas He that brought me to the fold,
'Tis He that still doth keep.

3 No more a wandering sheep,
I love to be controlled;
I love my tender Shepherd's voice,
I love, I love the fold.

4 No more a wayward child,
I seek no more to roam;
I love my heavenly Father's voice,
I love, I love His home!

268

1 Come, Lord, and tarry not,
Bring the long-looked-for day;
O why these years of waiting here,
These ages of delay!

2 Come! for the good are few,
They lift the voice in vain;
Faith waxes fainter on the earth,
And love is on the wane.

3 Come! for creation groans,
Impatient of Thy stay,
Worn out with these long years of ill,
These ages of delay.

4 Come, and make all things new;
Build up this ruined earth,
Restore our faded Paradise,
Creation's second birth!

5 Come, and begin Thy reign
Of everlasting peace;
Come, take the kingdom to Thyself,
Great King of Righteousness!

269
Psalm 122.

1 How pleased and blest was I
To hear the people cry,
"Come, let us seek our God to-day!"
Yes, with a cheerful zeal
We'll haste to Zion's hill,
And there our vows and honors pay.

2 Zion, thrice happy place,
Adorned with wondrous grace,
And walls of strength embrace thee round:
In Thee our tribes appear
To pray, and praise, and hear
The sacred gospel's joyful sound.

3 May peace attend thy gate,
And joy within thee wait
To bless the soul of every guest:
The man who seeks thy peace,
And wishes thine increase—
A thousand blessings on him rest!

4 My tongue repeats her vows,
"Peace to this sacred house!"
For here my friends and kindred dwell;
And since my glorious God
Makes thee His blest abode,
My soul shall ever love thee well.

270
Psalm 93.

1 The Lord Jehovah reigns,
And royal state maintains,
His head with awful glories crowned;
Arrayed in robes of light,
Begirt with sovereign might,
And rays of majesty around.

2 Upheld by Thy commands,
The world securely stands,
And skies and stars obey Thy word;
Thy throne was fixed on high
Before the starry sky;
Eternal is Thy kingdom, Lord!

3 Let floods and nations rage,
And all their power engage;
Let swelling tides assault the sky:
The terrors of Thy frown
Shall beat their madness down;
Thy throne forever stands on high.

4 Thy promises are true,
Thy grace is ever new;
There fixed, Thy church shall ne'er remove.
Thy saints, with holy fear,
Shall in Thy courts appear,
And sing Thine everlasting love.

271

1 How calm and beautiful the morn
That gilds the sacred tomb,
Where once the Crucified was borne,
And veiled in midnight gloom!
O weep no more the Saviour slain;
The Lord is risen—He lives again.

2 Ye mourning saints, dry every tear
For your departed Lord;
"Behold the place—He is not here,"
The tomb is all unbarred:
The gates of death were closed in vain;
The Lord is risen—He lives again.

3 Now cheerful to the house of prayer
Your early footsteps bend,
The Saviour will Himself be there,
Your advocate and friend:
Once by the law your hopes were slain,
But now in Christ ye live again.

4 How tranquil now the rising day!
'Tis Jesus still appears,
A risen Lord to chase away
Your unbelieving fears:
O weep no more your comforts slain,
The Lord is risen—He lives again.

5 And when the shades of evening fall,
When life's last hour draws nigh,
If Jesus shine upon the soul,
How blissful then to die:
Since He has risen who once was slain,
Ye die in Christ to live again.

272

1 Songs of praise the angels sang,
Heaven with hallelujahs rang,
When Jehovah's work begun,
When He spake, and it was done.

2 Songs of praise awoke the morn
When the Prince of Peace was born;
Songs of praise arose, when He
Captive led captivity.

3 Heaven and earth must pass away,
Songs of praise shall crown that day;
God will make new heavens and earth,
Songs of praise shall hail their birth.

4 Saints below, with heart and voice,
Still in songs of praise rejoice;
Learning here, by faith and love,
Songs of praise to sing above.

273 *Psalm 148.*

1 Heralds of creation, cry,
"Praise the Lord, the Lord most high;"
Heaven and earth, obey the call,
Praise the Lord, the Lord of all.

2 For He spake, and forth from night
Sprang the universe to light;
He commanded—nature heard,
And stood fast upon His word.

3 Praise Him, all ye hosts above;
Spirits perfected in love;
Sun and moon, your voices raise;
Sing, ye stars, your Maker's praise.

4 High above all height, His throne;
Excellent His name alone;
Him let all His works confess,
Him let all His children bless.

274 *Psalm 150.*

1 Praise the Lord, His glories show,
Saints within His courts below,
Angels round His throne above,
All that see and share His love.

2 Earth to heaven, and heaven to earth,
Tell His wonders, sing His worth;
Age to age, and shore to shore,
Praise Him, praise Him, evermore!

3 Praise the Lord, His mercies trace;
Praise His providence and grace,
All that He for man hath done,
All He sends us through His Son.

4 Strings and voices, hands and hearts,
In the concert bear your parts;
All that breathe, your Lord adore,
Praise Him, praise Him, evermore!

275

1 Angels, roll the rock away!
Death, yield up thy mighty prey!
See, the Saviour leaves the tomb,
Glowing with immortal bloom.

2 Hark! the wondering angels raise
Louder notes of joyful praise;
Let the earth's remotest bound
Echo with the blissful sound.

3 Saints on earth, lift up your eyes;
Now to glory see Him rise
In long triumph through the sky,
Up to waiting worlds on high.

4 Heaven unfolds its portals wide;
Mighty Conqueror, through them ride!
King of glory, mount Thy throne!
Boundless empire is Thine own.

276

1 Swell the anthem, raise the song;
Praises to our God belong;
Saints and angels, join to sing
Praises to the heavenly King.

2 Blessings from His liberal hand
Flow around this happy land;
Kept by Him, no foes annoy;
Peace and freedom we enjoy.

3 Here beneath a virtuous sway
May we cheerfully obey;
Never feel oppression's rod;
Ever own and worship God.

4 Hark! the voice of nature sings
Praises to the King of kings;
Let us join the choral song,
And the grateful notes prolong.

277

1 "Christ, the Lord, is risen to-day,"
Sons of men and angels say;
Raise your joys and triumphs high,
Sing, ye heavens, and earth reply.

2 Love's redeeming work is done,
Fought the fight, the battle won;
Lo, the sun's eclipse is o'er;
Lo, He sets in blood no more.

3 Vain the stone, the watch, the seal;
Christ hath burst the gates of hell!
Death in vain forbids Him rise;
Christ hath opened Paradise!

4 Lives again our glorious King;
Where, O death, is now thy sting!
Once He died, our souls to save;
Where's thy victory, boasting grave!

5 Soar we now where Christ has led,
Following our exalted Head;
Made like Him, like Him we rise;
Ours the cross, the grave, the skies.

278

1 Hark! the herald angels sing,
Glory to the new-born King!
Peace on earth, and mercy mild,
God and sinners reconciled!

2 Joyful, all ye nations, rise,
Join the triumph of the skies;
Universal nature say,
Christ the Lord is born to-day!

3 Hail! the heaven-born Prince of Peace!
Hail! the Sun of Righteousness!
Light and life to all He brings,
Risen with healing in His wings.

4 Mild He lays His glory by,
Born that man no more may die,
Born to raise the sons of earth,
Born to give them second birth.

279

1 Christ, the Lord, is risen to-day,
Our triumphant holy day;
He endured the cross and grave,
Sinners to redeem and save.

2 Lo, He rises, mighty King!
Where, O death, is now thy sting?
Lo, He claims His native sky!
Grave, where is thy victory!

3 Christ, the Lord, is risen to-day,
Our triumphant holy day;
Loud the song of victory raise;
Shout the great Redeemer's praise.

280

1 Now begin the heavenly theme,
Sing aloud in Jesus' name!
Ye, who His salvation prove,
Triumph in redeeming love.

2 Ye, who see the Father's grace
Beaming in the Saviour's face,
As to Canaan on ye move,
Praise and bless redeeming love.

3 Mourning souls, dry up your tears;
Banish all your guilty fears;
See your guilt and curse remove,
Cancelled by redeeming love.

4 Hither then your music bring,
Strike aloud each cheerful string;
Mortals, join the host above,
Join to praise redeeming love.

281

1 Hasten, Lord, the glorious time,
When, beneath Messiah's sway,
Every nation, every clime,
Shall the gospel call obey.

2 Mightiest kings His power shall own,
Heathen tribes His name adore;
Satan and his host, o'erthrown,
Bound in chains, shall hurt no more.

3 Then shall wars and tumults cease,
Then be banished grief and pain;
Righteousness, and joy, and peace,
Undisturbed shall ever reign.

4 Bless we, then, our gracious Lord;
Ever praise His glorious Name;
All His mighty acts record;
All His wondrous love proclaim.

282

1 Hark! that shout of rapturous joy,
  Bursting forth from yonder cloud!
  Jesus comes, and through the sky
  Angels tell their joy aloud.
  Hark! the trumpet's awful voice
  Sounds abroad through sea and land!
  Let His people now rejoice,
  Their redemption is at hand.

2 See! the Lord appears in view;
  Heaven and earth before Him fly:
  Rise, ye saints, He comes for you,
  Rise to meet Him in the sky:
  Go, and dwell with Him above
  Where no foe can e'er molest;
  Happy in the Saviour's love,
  Ever blessing, ever blest.

283

1 Hark! the song of jubilee,
  Loud as mighty thunders roar,
  Or the fulness of the sea,
  When it breaks upon the shore!
  Hallelujah! for the Lord
  God Omnipotent shall reign;
  Hallelujah! let the word
  Echo round the earth and main.

2 Hallelujah! hark! the sound,
  From the centre to the skies,
  Wakes above, beneath, around,
  All creation's harmonies.
  See Jehovah's banner furled,
  Sheathed His sword—He speaks, 'tis done;
  And the kingdoms of this world
  Are the kingdoms of His Son.

3 He shall reign from pole to pole,
  With illimitable sway;
  He shall reign, when like a scroll
  Yonder heavens have passed away;
  Then the end; beneath His rod
  Man's last enemy shall fall;
  Hallelujah! Christ in God,
  God in Christ, is all in all.

284

1 Hail, the day that sees Him rise,
  Ravished from our wishful eyes!
  Christ, awhile to mortals given,
  Reascends His native heaven:
  There the pompous triumph waits:
  "Lift your heads, eternal gates!
  Wide unfold the radiant scene,
  Take the King of Glory in!"

2 Him though highest heaven receives,
  Still He loves the earth He leaves;
  Though returning to His throne,
  Still He calls mankind His own:
  Still for us His death He pleads,
  Prevalent He intercedes,
  Near Himself prepares our place,
  Harbinger of human race.

3 Master, will we ever say,
  Taken from our head to-day,
  See Thy faithful servants, see,
  Ever gazing up to Thee!
  Grant, though parted from our sight,
  High above yon azure height;
  Grant, our hearts may thither rise,
  Following Thee beyond the skies!

285

1 Crowns of glory ever bright
  Rest upon the Conqueror's head;
  Crowns of glory are His right,
  His "who liveth and was dead."
  He subdued the powers of hell;
  In the fight He stood alone;
  All His foes before Him fell,
  By His single arm o'erthrown.

2 His the battle, His the toil,
  His the honors of the day,
  His the glory and the spoil;
  Jesus bears them all away:
  Now proclaim His deeds afar;
  Fill the world with His renown;
  His alone the victor's car,
  His the everlasting crown!

286*

1 Ask ye what great thing I know
That delights and stirs me so?
What the high reward I win?
Whose the name I glory in?
Jesus Christ the Crucified.

2 What is faith's foundation strong?
What awakes my lips to song?
He who bore my sinful load,
Purchased for me peace with God—
Jesus Christ, the Crucified.

3 Who is life in life to me?
Who the death of death will be?
Who will place me on His right
With the countless hosts of light?
Jesus Christ, the Crucified.

4 This is that great thing I know;
This delights and stirs me so;
Faith in Him who died to save,
Him who triumphed o'er the grave—
Jesus Christ, the Crucified.

287

1 Morning breaks upon the tomb;
Jesus scatters all its gloom;
Day of triumph! through the skies
See the glorious Saviour rise!

2 Christian, dry your flowing tears;
Chase those unbelieving fears
Look on His deserted grave;
Doubt no more His power to save.

3 Ye, who are of death afraid,
Triumph in the scattered shade;
Drive your anxious cares away;
See the place where Jesus lay.

4 Lo! the rising sun appears,
Shedding radiance o'er the spheres;
Lo! returning beams of light
Chase the terrors of the night.

288

1 Children of the heavenly King,
As ye journey sweetly sing;
Sing your Saviour's worthy praise,
Glorious in His works and ways.

* If this hymn be sung to "Flint," repeat first line of the tune.

2 Ye are travelling home to God
In the way the fathers trod;
They are happy now, and ye
Soon their happiness shall see.

3 Shout, ye little flock, and blest!
You on Jesus' throne shall rest;
There your seat is now prepared;
There your kingdom and reward.

4 Fear not, brethren; joyful stand
On the borders of your land;
Jesus Christ, your Father's Son,
Bids you undismayed go on.

289

1 High in yonder realms of light,
Dwell the raptured saints above,
Far beyond our feeble sight,
Happy in Immanuel's love.

2 'Mid the chorus of the skies,
'Mid the angelic lyres above,
Hark, their songs melodious rise,
Songs of praise to Jesus' love!

3 All is tranquil and serene,
Calm and undisturbed repose;
There no cloud can intervene,
There no angry tempest blows.

4 Every tear is wiped away,
Sighs no more shall heave the breast,
Night is lost in endless day,
Sorrow, in eternal rest.

290   Psalm 136.

1 Let us with a gladsome mind
Praise the Lord, for He is kind;
For His mercy shall endure
Ever faithful, ever sure.

2 He, with all-commanding might,
Filled the new-made world with light;
For His mercy shall endure
Ever faithful, ever sure.

3 All things living He doth feed,
His full hand supplies their need;
For His mercy shall endure
Ever faithful, ever sure.

4 Let us then with gladsome mind
Praise the Lord, for He is kind;
For His mercy shall endure
Ever faithful, ever sure.

291

1 What are these in bright array,
This innumerable throng,
Round the altar, night and day,
Hymning one triumphant song:
"Worthy is the Lamb, once slain,
Blessing, honor, glory, power,
Wisdom, riches, to obtain
New dominion every hour!"

2 These through fiery trials trod,
These from great affliction came;
Now, before the throne of God,
Sealed with His almighty name,
Clad in raiment pure and white,
Victor-palms in every hand,
Through their dear Redeemer's might,
More than conquerors they stand.

3 Hunger, thirst, disease unknown,
On immortal fruits they feed;
Them the Lamb amidst the throne
Shall to living fountains lead:
Joy and gladness banish sighs;
Perfect love dispels all fear;
And forever from their eyes
God shall wipe away the tear.

292

1 Come, ye thankful people, come,
Raise the song of harvest-home!
All is safely gathered in,
Ere the winter storms begin;
God our Maker doth provide
For our wants to be supplied:
Come to God's own temple, come,
Raise the song of harvest-home!

2 For the Lord our God shall come,
And shall take His harvest home;
From His field shall in that day
All offences purge away;
Give His angels charge at last
In the fire the tares to cast;
But the fruitful ears to store
In His garner evermore.

3 Even so, Lord, quickly come
To Thy final harvest-home!
Gather Thou Thy people in,
Free from sorrow, free from sin,
There, forever purified,
In Thy presence to abide:
Come, with all Thine angels, come,
Raise the glorious harvest-home!

293

1 Welcome, sacred day of rest!
Sweet repose from worldly care;
Day above all days the best,
When our souls for heaven prepare;
Day when our Redeemer rose,
Victor o'er the hosts of hell:
Thus He vanquished all our foes;
Let our lips His glory tell.

2 Gracious Lord! we love this day,
When we hear Thy holy word;
When we sing Thy praise, and pray,
Earth can no such joys afford;
But a better rest remains,
Heavenly Sabbaths, happier days;
Rest from sin, and rest from pains,
Endless joys, and endless praise.

294

1 Praise to God, immortal praise,
For the love that crowns our days!
Bounteous Source of every joy,
Let Thy praise our tongues employ.

2 For the blessings of the field,
For the stores the gardens yield,
For the joys which harvests bring,
Grateful praises now we sing.

3 All that spring with bounteous hand
Scatters o'er the smiling land;
All that liberal autumn pours
From her rich o'erflowing stores;

4 Lord, for these our souls shall raise
Grateful vows and solemn praise,
And when every blessing's flown,
Love Thee for Thyself alone.

295

1 From the cross uplifted high,
Where the Saviour deigns to die,
What melodious sounds we hear,
Bursting on the ravished ear!
"Love's redeeming work is done;
Come and welcome, sinner, come!

2 "Sprinkled now with blood the throne;
Why beneath thy burdens groan?
On my piercéd body laid,
Justice owns the ransom paid;
Bow the knee, and kiss the Son:
Come and welcome, sinner, come!

3 "Spread for thee, the festal board
See with richest dainties stored;
To thy Father's bosom pressed,
Yet again a child confessed,
Never from His house to roam:
Come and welcome, sinner, come!

4 "Soon the days of life shall end;
Lo I come, your Saviour, friend,
Safe your spirit to convey
To the realms of endless day,
Up to my eternal home:
Come and welcome, sinner, come!"

296

1 Blessed are the sons of God;
They are bought with Jesus' blood;
They are ransomed from the grave—
Life, eternal life they have:
With them numbered may we be,
Here and in eternity.

2 They are justified by grace;
They enjoy the Saviour's peace;
All their sins are washed away;
They shall stand in God's great day:
With them numbered may we be,
Here and in eternity.

3 They are lights upon the earth,
Children of a heavenly birth,
One with God, with Jesus one;
Glory is in them begun:
With them numbered may we be,
Here and in eternity.

297

1 Christ, whose glory fills the sky,
Christ, the true, the only light,
Sun of Righteousness, arise,
Triumph o'er the shades of night!
Day-spring from on high, be near!
Day-star, in my heart appear!

2 Dark and cheerless is the morn,
Unaccompanied by Thee;
Joyless is the day's return,
Till Thy mercy's beams I see;
Till they inward light impart,
Glad my eyes and warm my heart.

3 Visit, then, this soul of mine;
Pierce the gloom of sin and grief;
Fill me, Radiancy Divine!
Scatter all my unbelief;
More and more Thyself display,
Shining to the perfect day.

298

1 Blessed Saviour! Thee I love,
All my other joys above;
All my hopes in Thee abide,
Thou my hope, and naught beside:
Ever let my glory be,
Only, only, only Thee.

2 Once again beside the cross,
All my gain I count but loss;
Earthly pleasures fade away,
Clouds they are that hide my day:
Hence, vain shadows! let me see
Jesus crucified for me.

3 From beneath that thorny crown
Trickle drops of cleansing down;
Pardon from Thy piercéd hand
Now I take, while here I stand:
Only then I live to Thee,
When Thy wounded side I see.

4 Blesséd Saviour! Thine am I,
Thine to live, and Thine to die;
Height or depth, or earthly power
Ne'er shall hide my Saviour more:
Ever shall my glory be,
Only, only, only Thee!

299

1 Rock of Ages, cleft for me,
  Let me hide myself in Thee;
  Let the water and the blood,
  From Thy riven side which flowed,
  Be of sin the double cure,
  Cleanse me from its guilt and power.

2 Not the labors of my hands
  Can fulfil Thy law's demands:
  Could my zeal no respite know,
  Could my tears forever flow,
  All for sin could not atone;
  Thou must save, and Thou alone.

3 Nothing in my hand I bring;
  Simply to Thy cross I cling;
  Naked, come to Thee for dress;
  Helpless, look to Thee for grace;
  Foul, I to the Fountain fly;
  Wash me, Saviour, or I die!

4 While I draw this fleeting breath,
  When my eyelids close in death,
  When I soar to worlds unknown,
  See Thee on Thy judgment-throne,
  Rock of Ages, cleft for me,
  Let me hide myself in Thee.

300

1 As with gladness men of old
  Did the guiding star behold;
  As with joy they hailed its light,
  Leading onward, beaming bright;
  So, most gracious Lord, may we
  Evermore be led to Thee.

2 As with joyful steps they sped
  To that lowly manger-bed,
  There to bend the knee before
  Him whom heaven and earth adore;
  So may we with willing feet
  Ever seek the mercy-seat.

3 As they offered gifts most rare
  At that manger rude and bare;
  So may we with holy joy,
  Pure and free from sin's alloy,
  All our costliest treasures bring,
  Christ, to Thee, our heavenly King.

301

1 Safely through another week
  God has brought us on our way;
  Let us now a blessing seek,
  Waiting in His courts to-day;
  Day of all the week the best,
  Emblem of eternal rest.

2 While we pray for pardoning grace
  Through the dear Redeemer's name,
  Show Thy reconciléd face,
  Take away our sin and shame;
  From our worldly cares set free,
  May we rest this day in Thee.

3 Here we come Thy Name to praise;
  Let us feel Thy presence near;
  May Thy glory meet our eyes
  While we in Thy house appear:
  Here afford us, Lord, a taste
  Of our everlasting feast.

4 May Thy gospel's joyful sound
  Conquer sinners, comfort saints;
  Make the fruits of grace abound;
  Bring relief for all complaints:
  Thus let all our Sabbaths prove
  Till we rest in Thee above.

302   Psalm 67.

1 God of mercy, God of grace,
  Show the brightness of Thy face;
  Shine upon us, Saviour, shine,
  Fill Thy church with light divine,
  And Thy saving health extend
  To the earth's remotest end.

2 Let the people praise Thee, Lord,
  Be by all that live adored;
  Let the nations shout and sing
  Glory to their Saviour-King;
  At Thy feet their tribute pay,
  And Thy holy will obey.

3 Let the people praise Thee, Lord;
  Earth shall then her fruits afford,
  God to man His blessing give,
  Man to God devoted live;
  All below, and all above,
  One in joy and light and love.

CHRISTIAN PRAISE.

MARTYN. 7s. Double.

HOTHAM. 7s. Double.

WATCHMAN, TELL US OF THE NIGHT. 7s. Double.

Small notes in 1st measure used on D.C.

303

1 Jesus, Lover of my soul,
   Let me to Thy bosom fly,
   While the nearer waters roll,
   While the tempest still is high;
   Hide me, O my Saviour, hide,
   Till the storm of life be past;
   Safe into the haven guide;
   O receive my soul at last!

2 Other refuge have I none:
   Hangs my helpless soul on Thee;
   Leave, ah! leave me not alone,
   Still support and comfort me!
   All my trust on Thee is stayed,
   All my help from Thee I bring;
   Cover my defenceless head
   With the shadow of Thy wing!

3 Plenteous grace with Thee is found,
   Grace to cover all my sin;
   Let the healing streams abound;
   Make and keep me pure within!
   Thou of life the fountain art,
   Freely let me take of Thee;
   Spring Thou up within my heart!
   Rise to all eternity!

304

1 Watchman, tell us of the night,
   What its signs of promise are!
   Traveller, o'er yon mountain's height
   See that glory-beaming star!
   Watchman, does its beauteous ray
   Aught of joy or hope foretell?
   Traveller, yes; it brings the day,
   Promised day of Israel.

2 Watchman, tell us of the night;
   Higher yet that star ascends!
   Traveller, blessedness and light,
   Peace and truth its course portends!
   Watchman, will its beams alone
   Gild the spot that gave them birth?
   Traveller, ages are its own;
   See, it bursts o'er all the earth.

3 Watchman, tell us of the night;
   For the morning seems to dawn!
   Traveller, darkness takes its flight,
   Doubt and terror are withdrawn:
   Watchman, let thy wanderings cease;
   Hie thee to thy quiet home!
   Traveller, lo! the Prince of Peace,
   Lo! the Son of God is come!

305 [Hotham.]

1 Lord, from earthly cares set free,
   Let us find our rest in Thee:
   May our toils and conflicts cease
   In the calm of Sabbath peace;
   That Thy people here below
   Something of the bliss may know,
   Something of the rest and love,
   In the Sabbath home above.

2 From beyond the grave's dark night,
   What mild radiance meets my sight!
   Softly stealing on the ear,
   What strange music do I hear!
   'Tis the golden crown on high,
   'Tis the chorus of the sky!
   Lord, Thy sinful child prepare
   For a place and portion there.

306 [Watchman.]

1 Thou who art enthroned above,
   Thou in whom we live and move,
   Good it is with joyful tongue
   To resound Thy praise in song:
   When the morning paints the skies,
   When the sparkling stars arise,
   All Thy favors to rehearse,
   And give thanks in grateful verse.

2 Sweet the day of sacred rest,
   When devotion fires the breast,
   When we dwell within Thy house,
   Hear Thy gospel, pay our vows,
   Songs to heaven's high mansion raise,
   Fill Thy courts with songs of praise,
   And in psalms and hymns proclaim
   Honors to Thy glorious Name.

CHRISTIAN PRAISE.

NUREMBURG. 7s. 6 lines.

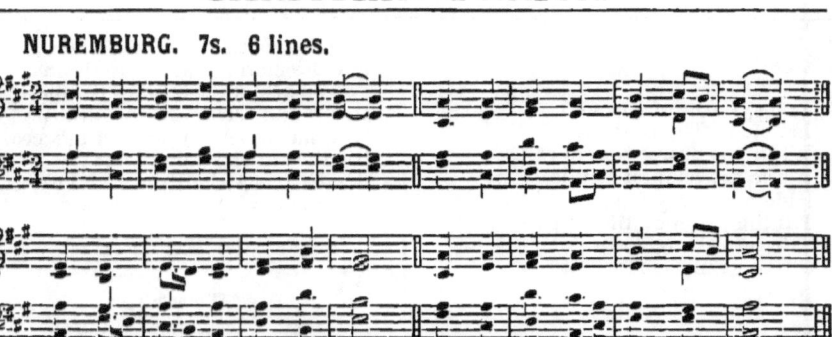

HANCHETT. 7s. 6 lines.

SWIFT. 7s. 6 lines.

307

1 Shepherd, with Thy tenderest love
Guide me to Thy fold above,
Let me hear Thy gentle voice,
More and more in Thee rejoice,
From Thy fulness grace receive,
Ever in Thy Spirit live.

2 Filled by Thee, my cup o'erflows,
For Thy love no limit knows;
Guardian angels, ever nigh,
Lead and draw my soul on high;
Constant to my latest end,
Thou my footsteps wilt attend.

3 Jesus, with Thy presence blest,
Death is life, and labor rest;
Guide me while I draw my breath,
Guard me through the gate of death,
And at last, O let me stand
With the sheep at Thy right hand.

308

1 Come to Calvary's holy mountain,
Sinners ruined by the fall;
Here a pure and healing fountain
Flows to you, to me, to all,
In a full, perpetual tide,
Opened when our Saviour died.

2 Come in sorrow and contrition,
Wounded, impotent, and blind;
Here the guilty, free remission,
Here the troubled, peace may find;
Health this fountain will restore,
He that drinks shall thirst no more.

3 He that drinks shall live forever;
'Tis a soul-renewing flood;
God is faithful, God will never
Break His covenant in blood;
Signed when our Redeemer died,
Sealed when He was glorified.

309

1 Now from labor and from care
Evening shades have set me free:
In the work of praise and prayer,
Lord, I would converse with Thee;
O behold me from above;
Fill me with a Saviour's love!

2 Sin and sorrow, guilt and woe,
Wither all my earthly joys;
Naught can charm me here below
But my Saviour's melting voice;
Lord, forgive, Thy grace restore;
Make me Thine for evermore!

3 For the blessings of this day,
For the mercies of this hour,
For the Gospel's cheering ray,
For the Spirit's quickening power,
Grateful notes to Thee I raise;
O accept my song of praise!

310

1 In this calm, impressive hour,
Let my prayer ascend on high:
God of mercy, God of power,
Hear me, when to Thee I cry;
Hear me from Thy lofty throne,
For the sake of Christ Thy Son.

2 With the morning's early ray,
While the shades of night depart,
Let Thy beams of light convey
Joy and gladness to my heart:
Now o'er all my steps preside,
And for all my wants provide.

3 O what joy that word affords:
"Thou shalt reign o'er all the earth;"
King of kings, and Lord of lords,
Send Thy gospel heralds forth;
Now begin Thy boundless sway,
Usher in the glorious day!

311

1 Light of Light, enlighten me!
Now anew the day is dawning;
Sun of grace, the shadows flee,
Brighten Thou my Sabbath morning!
With Thy joyous sunshine blest,
Happy is my day of rest.

2 Fount of all our joy and peace,
To Thy living waters lead me;
Thou from earth my soul release,
And with grace and mercy feed me;
Bless Thy word that it may prove
Rich in fruits that Thou dost love.

312

1 Light of life, seraphic fire;
  Love divine, Thyself impart:
  Every fainting soul inspire;
  Shine in every drooping heart.

2 Every mournful sinner cheer,
  Scatter all our guilty gloom;
  Son of God, appear, appear!
  To Thy human temples come!

3 Come, in this accepted hour,
  Bring Thy heavenly kingdom in;
  Fill us with the glorious power
  Rooting out the seeds of sin.

4 Nothing more can we require,
  We will covet nothing less;
  Be Thou all our heart's desire,
  All our joy and all our peace!

313

1 When on Sinai's top I see
  God descend in majesty,
  To proclaim His holy law,
  All my spirit sinks with awe.

2 When in ecstasy sublime,
  Tabor's glorious steep I climb,
  At the too transporting light
  Darkness rushes o'er my sight.

3 When on Calvary I rest,
  God in flesh made manifest,
  Shines in my Redeemer's face,
  Full of beauty, truth, and grace.

4 Here I would forever stay,
  Weep and gaze my soul away;
  Thou art heaven on earth to me,
  Lovely, mournful Calvary.

314

1 Christ, of all my hopes the ground,
  Christ, the spring of all my joy,
  Still in Thee let me be found,
  Still for Thee my powers employ.

2 Fountain of o'erflowing grace,
  Freely from Thy fulness give;
  Till I close my earthly race,
  Be it "Christ for me to live."

3 When I touch the blessed shore,
  Back the closing waves shall roll;
  Death's dark stream shall never more
  Part from Thee my ravished soul.

4 Thus, O thus, an entrance give
  To the land of cloudless sky!
  Having known it "Christ to live,"
  Let me know it "gain to die."

315 Psalm 23.

1 To Thy pastures, fair and large,
  Heavenly Shepherd, lead Thy charge,
  And my couch, with tenderest care,
  'Mid the springing grass prepare.

2 When I faint with summer's heat,
  Thou shalt guide my weary feet
  To the streams that, still and slow,
  Through the verdant meadows flow.

3 Safe the dreary vale I tread,
  By the shades of death o'erspread,
  With Thy rod and staff supplied,
  This my guard, and that my guide.

4 Constant to my latest end,
  Thou my footsteps shalt attend;
  And shalt bid Thy hallowed dome
  Yield me an eternal home.

316

1 Cast thy burden on the Lord,
  Only lean upon His word;
  Thou wilt soon have cause to bless
  His unchanging faithfulness.

2 He sustains thee by His hand,
  He enables thee to stand;
  Those whom Jesus once hath loved
  From His grace are never moved.

3 Heaven and earth may pass away,
  God's free grace shall not decay;
  He hath promised to fulfil
  All the pleasure of His will.

4 Jesus, guardian of Thy flock,
  Be Thyself our constant rock;
  Make us by Thy powerful hand
  Firm as Zion's mountain stand.

317

1 Holy Ghost, with light divine,
  Shine upon this heart of mine;
  Chase the shades of night away,
  Turn my darkness into day.

2 Holy Ghost, with power divine,
  Cleanse this guilty heart of mine;
  Long hath sin, without control,
  Held dominion o'er my soul.

3 Holy Ghost, with joy divine,
  Cheer this saddened heart of mine;
  Bid my many woes depart,
  Heal my wounded, bleeding heart.

4 Holy Spirit, All-divine,
  Dwell within this heart of mine;
  Cast down every idol-throne,
  Reign supreme, and reign alone.

318

1 Lord, we come before Thee now,
  At Thy feet we humbly bow;
  O do not our suit disdain;
  Shall we seek Thee, Lord, in vain?

2 Lord, on Thee our souls depend;
  In compassion now descend;
  Fill our hearts with Thy rich grace,
  Tune our lips to sing Thy praise.

3 In Thine own appointed way
  Now we seek Thee, here we stay;
  Lord, we know not how to go
  Till a blessing Thou bestow.

4 Send some message, from Thy word,
  That may joy and peace afford;
  Let Thy Spirit now impart
  Full salvation to each heart.

319

1 Bread of heaven, on Thee we feed,
  For Thy flesh is meat indeed;
  Ever let our souls be fed
  With this true and living bread!

2 Vine of heaven, Thy blood supplies
  This blest cup of sacrifice;
  Lord, Thy wounds our healing give,
  To Thy cross we look and live.

3 Day by day, with strength supplied
  Through the life of Him who died,
  Lord of life, O let us be
  Rooted, grafted, built in Thee!

320

1 Gracious Spirit, Dove divine,
  Let Thy light within me shine;
  All my guilty fears remove,
  Fill me with Thy heavenly love.

2 Speak Thy pardoning grace to me,
  Set the burdened sinner free,
  Lead me to the Lamb of God,
  Wash me in His precious blood.

3 Life and peace to me impart,
  Seal salvation on my heart,
  Breathe Thyself into my breast,
  Earnest of immortal rest.

4 Let me never from Thee stray,
  Keep me in the narrow way,
  Fill my soul with joy divine,
  Keep me, Lord, forever Thine.

321

1 Softly now the light of day
  Fades upon my sight away;
  Free from care, from labor free,
  Lord, I would commune with Thee!

2 Thou whose all-pervading eye
  Naught escapes without, within,
  Pardon each infirmity,
  Open fault and secret sin!

3 Soon, for me, the light of day
  Shall forever pass away;
  Then, from sin and sorrow free,
  Take me, Lord, to dwell with Thee!

322

1 Come, my soul, thy suit prepare,
  Jesus loves to answer prayer;
  He Himself has bid thee pray,
  Therefore will not say thee nay.

2 Lord, I come to Thee for rest,
  Take possession of my breast;
  There Thy blood-bought right maintain,
  And without a rival reign.

3 While I am a pilgrim here,
  Let Thy love my spirit cheer;
  As my guide, my guard, my friend,
  Lead me to my journey's end.

4 Show me what I have to do,
  Every hour my strength renew;
  Let me live a life of faith,
  Let me die Thy people's death.

CHRISTIAN PRAISE.

HOLLEY. 7s.

MOUNT CALVARY. 7s. 6 lines.

QUIMBY. 7s. Double.

323

1 Son of God, to Thee I cry!
   By the holy mystery
   Of Thy dwelling here on earth,
   By Thy pure and holy birth,
   Hear, O hear my lowly plea;
   Manifest Thyself to me!

2 Lamb of God, to Thee I cry!
   By Thy bitter agony,
   By Thy pangs to us unknown,
   By Thy spirit's parting groan,
   Hear, O hear my lowly plea;
   Manifest Thyself to me!

3 Lord of glory, God most high,
   Man exalted to the sky,
   With Thy love my bosom fill;
   Prompt me to perform Thy will:
   Then Thy glory I shall see;
   Thou wilt bring me home to Thee.

324

1 Many woes had Christ endured,
   Many sore temptations met,
   Patient, and to pains inured;
   But the sorest trial yet
   Was to be sustained in thee,
   Gloomy, sad Gethsemane.

2 Came at length the dreadful night,
   Vengeance with its iron rod
   Stood, and with collected might
   Bruised the harmless Lamb of God:
   See, my soul, the Saviour see
   Prostrate in Gethsemane.

3 Here's my claim, and here alone;
   None a Saviour more can need;
   Deeds of righteousness I've none;
   Not a work that I can plead;
   Not a glimpse of hope for me—
   Only in Gethsemane.

4 Father, Son, and Holy Ghost,
   One Almighty God of love,
   Praised by all the heavenly host,
   In Thy shining courts above,
   We poor sinners, gracious Three
   Praise Thee for Gethsemane.

325 [Holley.]

1 Father, while we break this bread,
   And our Lord remember thus,
   Make us one with Him, our Head,
   Thou in Him, and He in us.

2 While to lips with praise that glow,
   This communion cup we press,
   Holy Father, make us grow
   More like Him we thus confess.

3 Reconciled in Christ, Thy Son,
   In whose name on Thee we call;
   Make us perfect, all in one,
   We in Him, and Thou in all.

326 [Quimby.]

1 Saviour, when in dust to Thee
   Low we bend the adoring knee;
   When repentant, to the skies
   Scarce we lift our weeping eyes;
   O by all the pains and woe
   Suffered once for man below,
   Bending from Thy throne on high,
   Hear our solemn litany!

2 By Thine hour of dire despair,
   By Thine agony of prayer,
   By the cross, the nail, the thorn,
   Piercing spear, and torturing scorn,
   By the gloom that veiled the skies
   O'er the dreadful sacrifice,
   Listen to our humble cry,
   Hear our solemn litany!

3 By Thy deep expiring groan,
   By the sad sepulchral stone,
   By the vault whose dark abode
   Held in vain the rising God,
   O from earth to heaven restored,
   Mighty, re-ascended Lord,
   Listen, listen to the cry
   Of our solemn litany!

327 [Benevento.]

1 While with ceaseless course the sun
Hasted through the former year,
Many souls their race have run,
Nevermore to meet us here:
Fixed in an eternal state,
They have done with all below;
We a little longer wait,
But how little none can know.

2 As the wingéd arrow flies
Speedily the mark to find;
As the lightning from the skies
Darts, and leaves no trace behind;
Swiftly thus our fleeting days
Bear us down life's rapid stream:
Upward, Lord, our spirits raise,
All below is but a dream.

3 Thanks for mercies past receive;
Pardon of our sins renew;
Teach us, henceforth, how to live
With eternity in view:
Bless Thy word to young and old;
Fill us with a Saviour's love;
And when life's short tale is told,
May we dwell with Thee above.

328

1 God, most mighty, sovereign Lord,
By the heavenly hosts adored,
God of nations, King of kings,
Head of all created things;
By Thy saints with joy confest,
God o'er all forever blest:
Lo! we come before Thy throne
In our Saviour's name alone.

2 On our fields of grass and grain,
Drop, O Lord, the kindly rain;
O'er our wide and goodly land,
Crown the labors of each hand;
Let Thy kind protection be
O'er our commerce on the sea;
Open, Lord, Thy bounteous hand,
Bless Thy people, bless our land.

3 Let, O Lord, our rulers be
Men that love and honor Thee;
Let the powers by Thee ordained,
Be in righteousness maintained;
In the people's hearts increase
Love of piety and peace;
Thus, united we shall stand,
One wide, free, and happy land.

4 God the Father, let Thy love
Shine upon us from above;
God the Son, our Saviour, plead,
With Thy blood, for all we need;
God the Holy Ghost, impart
Healing power to every heart;
Triune God, O hear our plea,
Save us as we trust in Thee.

329 [Ellery.]

1 The God of Abraham praise,
Who reigns enthroned above,
Ancient of everlasting days,
And God of love!
Jehovah! Great I AM!
By earth and heaven confest;
I bow and bless the sacred name,
Forever blest!

2 The God who reigns on high,
The great archangels sing,
And "Holy, holy, holy," cry,
"Almighty King!
Who was, who is, the same,
And evermore shall be!"
Jehovah! Father! Great I AM!
We worship Thee!

3 The whole triumphant host
Give thanks to God on high;
"Hail! Father, Son, and Holy Ghost!"
They ever cry;
Hail! Abraham's God, and mine!
I join the heavenly lays;
All might and majesty are Thine,
And endless praise!

4 The God of Abraham praise,
At whose supreme command
From earth I rise, and seek the joys
At His right hand:
I all on earth forsake,
Its wisdom, fame, and power;
And Him my only portion make,
My shield and tower.

330
Psalm 87.

1 Glorious things of Thee are spoken,
Zion, city of our God;
He whose word cannot be broken,
Formed thee for His own abode;
On the Rock of Ages founded,
What can shake thy sure repose!
With salvation's walls surrounded,
Thou mayst smile at all thy foes.

2 See, the streams of living waters,
Springing from eternal love,
Well supply Thy sons and daughters,
And all fear of want remove;
Who can faint, while such a river
Ever flows their thirst to assuage!
Grace which, like the Lord the giver,
Never fails from age to age.

3 Round each habitation hovering,
See the cloud and fire appear
For a glory and a covering,
Showing that the Lord is near:
Thus deriving from their banner
Light by night and shade by day,
Safe they feed upon the manna
Which He gives them when they pray.

331

1 Lord, with glowing heart I'd praise Thee
For the bliss Thy love bestows,
For the pardoning grace that saves me,
And the peace that from it flows;
Help, O God, my weak endeavor;
This dull soul to rapture raise;
Thou must light the flame, or never
Can my love be warmed to praise.

2 Lord, this bosom's ardent feeling
Vainly would my lips express;
Low before Thy footstool kneeling,
Deign Thy suppliant's prayer to bless;
Let Thy grace, my soul's chief treasure,
Love's pure flame within me raise;
And since words can never measure,
Let my life show forth Thy praise.

332

1 Hail, my ever blessèd Jesus!
Only Thee I wish to sing;
To my soul Thy name is precious,
Thou my prophet, priest, and king;
O what mercy flows from heaven!
O what joy and happiness!
Love I much, I've much forgiven;
I'm a miracle of grace!

2 Once with Adam's race in ruin,
Unconcerned, in sin I lay;
Swift destruction still pursuing,
Till my Saviour passed that way;
Witness, all ye hosts of heaven,
My Redeemer's tenderness!
Love I much, I've much forgiven;
I'm a miracle of grace!

3 Shout, ye bright angelic choir!
Praise the Lamb enthroned above,
While, astonished, I admire
God's free grace and boundless love;
That blest moment I received Him
Filled my soul with joy and peace;
Love I much, I've much forgiven;
I'm a miracle of grace!

333

1 Take, my soul, thy full salvation;
Rise o'er sin, and fear, and care;
Joy to find, in every station,
Something still to do or bear;
Think what Spirit dwells within Thee!
Think what Father's smile is thine!
Think what Saviour died to win thee!
Child of heaven, shouldst thou repine?

2 Haste then on from grace to glory,
Armed by faith, and winged by prayer;
Heaven's eternal day 's before thee,
God's own hand shall guide thee there;
Soon shall close thine earthly mission,
Swift shall pass thy pilgrim days;
Hope shall change to glad fruition,
Faith to sight, and prayer to praise.

334
Psalm 148.

1 Praise the Lord! ye heavens, adore Him;
Praise Him, angels in the height;
Sun and moon, rejoice before Him;
Praise Him, all ye stars of light.

2 Praise the Lord, for He hath spoken,
Worlds His mighty voice obeyed;
Laws which never shall be broken,
For their guidance He hath made.

3 Praise the Lord, for He is glorious;
Never shall His promise fail;
God hath made His saints victorious,
Sin and death shall not prevail.

4 Praise the God of our salvation;
Hosts on high, His power proclaim;
Heaven and earth, and all creation,
Laud and magnify His name.

335

1 Hark! what mean those holy voices,
Sweetly sounding through the skies?
Lo, the angelic host rejoices;
Heavenly hallelujahs rise.

2 Hear them tell the wondrous story,
Hear them chant in hymns of joy,
"Glory in the highest, glory!
Glory be to God most high!"

3 "Peace on earth, good-will from heaven,
Reaching far as man is found;
Souls redeemed, and sin forgiven!
Loud our golden harps shall sound.

4 "Christ is born, the great Anointed;
Heaven and earth His praises sing!
O receive Whom God appointed
For your prophet, priest, and king!

5 "Haste, ye mortals, to adore Him,
Learn His name, and taste His joy,
Till in heaven ye sing before Him,
Glory be to God most high!"

336

1 Round the Lord in glory seated,
Cherubim and seraphim
Filled His temple and repeated
Each to each the alternate hymn:

2 "Lord, Thy glory fills the heaven,
Earth is with its fulness stored;
Unto Thee be glory given,
Holy, holy, holy Lord!"

3 Thus, Thy glorious name confessing,
We adopt the angels' cry,
"Holy, holy, holy"—blessing
Thee, the Lord our God most High!

4 Heaven is still with glory ringing;
Earth takes up the angels' cry,
"Holy, holy, holy," singing,
"Lord of hosts, the Lord most high."

5 With His seraph train before Him,
With His holy church below,
Thus conspire we to adore Him,
Bid we thus our anthem flow:

6 "Lord, Thy glory fills the heaven,
Earth is with its fulness stored;
Unto Thee be glory given,
Holy, holy, holy Lord!"

337

1 To the source of every blessing,
Grateful anthems let us raise;
Holy joy, our souls possessing,
Swells the tribute of our praise.

2 Glory to th' almighty Father,
Fountain of eternal love,
Who, His wandering sheep to gather,
Sent a Saviour from above.

3 To the Son all praise be given,
Who, with love unknown before,
Left the bright abode of heaven,
And our sins and sorrow bore.

4 Equal strains of warm devotion
Let the Spirit's praise employ;
Author of each pure emotion,
Source of wisdom, peace, and joy.

5 Thus our joyful hearts ascending,
Glorify Jehovah's name:
Heavenly songs with ours are blending,
There the theme is still the same.

338

1 In the cross of Christ I glory;
Towering o'er the wrecks of time,
All the light of sacred story
Gathers round its head sublime.

2 When the woes of life o'ertake me,
Hopes deceive, and fears annoy,
Never shall the cross forsake me;
Lo! it glows with peace and joy.

3 When the sun of bliss is beaming
Light and love upon my way,
From the cross the radiance streaming
Adds new lustre to the day.

4 Bane and blessing, pain and pleasure,
By the cross are sanctified;
Peace is there, that knows no measure,
Joys that through all time abide.

5 In the cross of Christ I glory;
Towering o'er the wrecks of time,
All the light of sacred story
Gathers round its head sublime.

339

1 Jesus, hail! enthroned in glory,
There forever to abide;
All the heavenly hosts adore Thee,
Seated at Thy Father's side.

2 There for sinners Thou art pleading;
There Thou dost our place prepare,
Ever for us interceding,
Till in glory we appear.

3 Worship, honor, power, and blessing,
Thou art worthy to receive;
Loudest praises without ceasing,
Meet it is for us to give.

4 Help, ye bright angelic spirits,
Bring your sweetest, noblest lays;
Help to sing our Saviour's merits,
Help to chant Immanuel's praise!

340

1 Hark, the sound of holy voices
Chanting at the crystal sea,
Hallelujah, hallelujah,
Hallelujah! Lord, to Thee.

2 Multitudes which none can number,
Like the stars in glory, stand
Clothed in white apparel, holding
Victor-palms in every hand.

3 They have come from tribulation,
And have washed their robes in blood,
Washed them in the blood of Jesus;
Tried they were, and firm they stood.

4 Gladly, Lord, with Thee they suffered,
Gladly, Lord, with Thee they died;
And, by death, to life immortal
They were born, and glorified.

5 Now they reign in heavenly glory,
Now they walk in golden light,
Now they drink, as from a river,
Holy bliss and infinite.

341

1 In the name of God the Father,
In the name of God the Son,
In the name of God the Spirit,
One in Three, and Three in one;

2 In the name which highest angels
Speak not ere they veil their face,
Crying, Holy, holy, holy,
Come we to this sacred place.

3 Lo, in wondrous condescension,
Jesus stoops from His high throne,
Though in lively symbols hidden,
Faith and love His presence own.

4 When the Lord His temple visits,
Let the listening earth be still;
May the Spirit's sweet indwelling
Each believing bosom fill.

5 Here shall highest praise be offered,
Here shall meekest prayer be poured,
Here, with body, soul, and spirit,
God incarnate be adored.

6 Holy Jesus, for Thy coming,
May Thy love our hearts prepare;
Thine we fain would have them wholly,
Enter, Lord, and tarry there.

342

1 Love divine, all love excelling,
  Joy of heaven, to earth come down,
  Fix in us Thy humble dwelling,
  All Thy faithful mercies crown!
  Jesus, Thou art all compassion;
  Pure, unbounded love, Thou art!
  Visit us with Thy salvation,
  Enter every trembling heart.

2 Breathe, O breathe Thy loving Spirit
  Into every troubled breast;
  Let us all in Thee inherit,
  Let us find Thy promised rest:
  Take away the love of sinning,
  Alpha and Omega be;
  End of faith, as its beginning,
  Set our hearts at liberty.

3 Come, Almighty to deliver,
  Let us all Thy life receive!
  Suddenly return, and never,
  Never more Thy temples leave!
  Thee we would be always blessing
  Serve Thee as Thy hosts above;
  Pray, and praise Thee without ceasing,
  Glory in Thy perfect love.

343

1 Jesus spreads His banner o'er us,
  Cheers our famished souls with food,
  He the banquet spreads before us
  Of His mystic flesh and blood:
  Precious banquet, bread of heaven!
  Wine of gladness, flowing free!
  May we taste it, kindly given,
  In remembrance, Lord, of Thee.

2 In Thy holy incarnation,
  When the angels sang Thy birth,
  In Thy fasting and temptation,
  In Thy labors on the earth,
  In Thy trial and rejection,
  In Thy suffering on the tree,
  In Thy glorious resurrection,
  May we, Lord, remember Thee.

344

1 Jesus, full of all compassion,
  Hear Thy humble suppliant's cry;
  Let me know Thy great salvation;
  See, I languish, faint, and die;
  Guilty, but with heart relenting,
  Overwhelmed with helpless grief,
  Prostrate at Thy feet repenting,
  Send, O send me quick relief.

2 Whither should a wretch be flying,
  But to Him who comfort gives!
  Whither, from the dread of dying,
  But to Him who ever lives!
  Saved! the deed shall spread new glory
  Through the shining realms above;
  Angels sing the pleasing story,
  All enraptured with Thy love.

345

1 Hail, Thou once despiséd Jesus!
  Hail, Thou Galilean King!
  Thou didst suffer to release us;
  Thou didst free salvation bring;
  Hail! Thou agonizing Saviour,
  Bearer of our sin and shame!
  By Thy merits we find favor;
  Life is givén through Thy name.

2 Paschal Lamb, by God appointed,
  All our sins on Thee were laid;
  By Almighty love anointed,
  Thou hast full atonement made;
  All Thy people are forgivén
  Through the virtue of Thy blood;
  Opened is the gate of heaven,
  Peace is made 'twixt man and God.

346

Praise the God of all creation;
Praise the Father's boundless love;
Praise the Lamb, our expiation,
Priest and King enthroned above:
Praise the fountain of salvation,
Him by whom our spirits live;
Undivided adoration
To the one Jehovah give.

347

1 Sweet the moments, rich in blessing,
Which before the cross I spend,
Life, and health, and peace possessing
From the sinner's dying Friend.

2 Here I'll sit, forever viewing
Mercy's streams in streams of blood;
Precious drops! my soul bedewing,
Plead, and claim my peace with God.

3 Truly blessèd is this station,
Low before His cross to lie,
While I see divine compassion
Floating in His languid eye.

4 Here it is I find my heaven
While upon the Lamb I gaze;
Here I see my sins forgiven,
Lost in wonder, love, and praise.

348

1 Come, Thou fount of every blessing,
Tune my heart to sing Thy grace;
Streams of mercy never ceasing,
Call for songs of loudest praise.

2 Jesus sought me when a stranger
Wandering from the fold of God;
He, to save my soul from danger,
Interposed His precious blood.

3 O to grace how great a debtor,
Daily I'm constrained to be!
Let that grace, Lord, like a fetter,
Bind my wandering heart to Thee.

4 Prone to wander, Lord, I feel it,
Prone to leave the God I love;
Here's my heart, O take and seal it,
Seal it from Thy courts above.

349

1 Saviour, breathe an evening blessing
Ere repose our eyelids seal;
Sin and want we come confessing;
Thou canst save and Thou canst heal.

2 Though destruction walk around us,
Though the arrows past us fly,
Angel-guards from Thee surround us;
We are safe if Thou art nigh.

3 Though the night be dark and dreary,
Darkness cannot hide from Thee;
Thou art He who, never weary,
Watchest where Thy people be.

4 Should swift death this night o'ertake us,
And our couch become our tomb,
May the morn in heaven awake us,
Clad in bright and deathless bloom.

350   Psalm 127

1 Vainly through night's weary hours,
Keep we watch lest foes alarm;
Vain our bulwarks and our towers
But for God's protecting arm.

2 Vain were all our toil and labor,
Did not God that labor bless;
Vain, without His grace and favor,
Every talent we possess.

3 Vainer still the hope of heaven,
That on human strength relies;
But to him shall help be given,
Who in humble faith applies.

4 Seek we, then, the Lord's Anointed,
He will grant us peace and rest;
Ne'er was suppliant disappointed,
Who to Christ his prayer addressed.

351

1 Saviour, who Thy flock art feeding
With the Shepherd's kindest care,
All the feeble gently leading,
While the lambs Thy bosom share;

2 Now, these little ones receiving,
Fold them in Thy gracious arm;
There we know, Thy word believing,
Only there, secure from harm.

3 Never, from Thy pasture roving,
Let them be the lion's prey;
Let Thy tenderness so loving
Keep them all life's dangerous way.

4 Then, within Thy fold eternal,
Let them find a resting-place,
Feed in pastures ever vernal,
Drink the rivers of Thy grace.

352

1 Gently, Lord, O gently lead us
Through this gloomy vale of tears;
Through the changes Thou'st decreed
Till our last great change appears. [us,

2 When temptation's darts assail us,
When in devious paths we stray,
Let Thy goodness never fail us,
Lead us in Thy perfect way.

3 In the hour of pain and anguish,
In the hour when death draws near,
Suffer not our hearts to languish,
Suffer not our souls to fear.

4 When this mortal life is ended,
Bid us in Thine arms to rest,
Till, by angel-bands attended,
We awake among the blest.

353

1 In this world of sin and sorrow,
Compassed round with every care,
From eternity we borrow
Hope that banishes despair.

2 Thee, triumphant God and Saviour,
In the glass of faith we see;
O assist each faint endeavor,
Raise our earth-born souls to Thee!

3 Bring that awful scene before us
Of the last tremendous day,
When to life Thou wilt restore us!
Lingering ages, haste away!

4 Then this vile and sinful nature
Incorruption shall put on;
Life-renewing, glorious Saviour,
Let Thy gracious will be done!

354

1 One there is, above all others,
Well deserves the name of friend;
His is love beyond a brother's,
Costly, free, and knows no end.

2 Which of all our friends, to save us,
Could or would have shed his blood!
But our Jesus died to have us
Reconciled in Him to God.

3 When He lived on earth abased,
Friend of sinners was His name;
Now, above all glory raised,
He rejoices in the same.

4 O for grace our hearts to soften!
Teach us, Lord, at length to love!
We, alas! forget too often
What a friend we have above.

355

1 Jesus, I my cross have taken,
All to leave, and follow Thee;
Destitute, despised, forsaken,
Thou, from hence, my all shalt be.

2 Perish every fond ambition,
All I've sought, or hoped, or known;
Yet how rich is my condition,
God and heaven are still my own!

3 Let the world despise and leave me,
They have left my Saviour too;
Human hearts and looks deceive me;
Thou art not, like them, untrue.

4 And while Thou shalt smile upon me,
God of wisdom, love, and might,
Foes may hate, and friends may shun me,
Show Thy face, and all is bright.

5 Go then, earthly fame and treasure!
Come disaster, scorn, and pain!
In Thy service pain is pleasure,
With Thy favor loss is gain.

6 I have called Thee Abba, Father,
I have stayed my heart on Thee;
Storms may howl and clouds may gather,
All must work for good to me.

7 Man may trouble and distress me,
'Twill but drive me to Thy breast;
Life with trials hard may press me,
Heaven will bring me sweeter rest.

8 O 'tis not in grief to harm me,
While Thy love is left to me;
O 'twere not in joy to charm me,
Were that joy unmixed with Thee.

356 [Harwell.]

1 Hark! ten thousand harps and voices
Sound the note of praise above;
Jesus reigns, and heaven rejoices;
Jesus reigns, the God of love;
See, He sits on yonder throne!
Jesus rules the world alone.

2 Jesus, hail! whose glory brightens
All above and gives it worth;
Lord of life, Thy smile enlightens,
Cheers and charms Thy saints on earth:
When we think of love like Thine,
Lord, we own it love divine.

3 King of glory, reign forever!
Thine an everlasting crown;
Nothing from Thy love shall sever
Those whom Thou hast made Thine own;
Happy objects of Thy grace,
Chosen to behold Thy face.

4 Saviour, hasten Thine appearing!
Bring, O bring the glorious day,
When the awful summons hearing,
Heaven and earth shall pass away!
Then with golden harps we'll sing,
"Glory, glory, to our King!"

357 Psalm 91.

1 Keep us, Lord, O keep us ever;
Vain our hope, if left by Thee;
We are Thine, O leave us never
Till Thy glorious face we see—
Then to praise Thee
Through a bright eternity.

2 Precious is Thy word of promise,
Precious to Thy people here;
Never take Thy presence from us,
Jesus, Saviour, still be near;
Living, dying,
May Thy name our spirits cheer.

358 Psalm 91. [Flint.]

1 Call Jehovah thy salvation,
Rest beneath the Almighty's shade;
In His secret habitation
Dwell, nor ever be dismayed.

2 There no tumult can alarm thee,
Thou shalt dread no hidden snare;
Guile nor violence can harm thee,
In eternal safeguard there.

3 He shall charge His angel-legions
Watch and ward o'er Thee to keep;
Though thou walk through hostile regions,
Though in desert wilds thou sleep.

4 Since with firm and pure affection
Thou on God hast set thy love,
With the wings of His protection
He will shield thee from above.

5 Thou shalt call on Him in trouble,
He will hearken, He will save;
Here for grief reward thee double
Crown with life beyond the grave.

359 [Flint.]

1 Come, Thou long-expected Jesus,
Born to set Thy people free;
From our fears and sins release us,
Let us find our rest in Thee.

2 Israel's strength and consolation,
Hope of all the earth Thou art;
Dear desire of every nation,
Joy of every longing heart.

3 Born Thy people to deliver
Born a Child, and yet a King,
Born to reign in us forever,
Now Thy gracious kingdom bring.

4 By Thine own eternal Spirit,
Rule in all our hearts alone;
By Thine all-sufficient merit,
Raise us to Thy glorious throne.

360 [Wilson.]

1 Our blest Redeemer, ere He breathed
His tender last farewell,
A guide, a comforter bequeathed
With us to dwell.

2 He came sweet influence to impart,
A gracious, willing guest,
While He can find one humble heart
Wherein to rest.

3 And every virtue we possess,
And every conquest won,
And every thought of holiness,
Are His alone.

4 Spirit of purity and grace,
Our weakness, pitying, see;
O make our hearts Thy dwelling-place,
And worthier Thee.

361

1 Look, ye saints, the sight is glorious;
See the Man of sorrows now
From the fight returned victorious!
Every knee to Him shall bow;
  Crown Him! Crown Him!
Crowns become the Victor's brow.

2 Crown the Saviour, angels, crown Him!
Rich the trophies Jesus brings;
In the seat of power enthrone Him
While the vault of heaven rings:
  Crown Him! Crown Him!
Crown the Saviour King of kings!

3 Sinners in derision crowned Him,
Mocking thus the Saviour's claim;
Saints and angels crowd around Him,
Own His title, praise His name!
  Crown Him! Crown Him!
Spread abroad the Victor's fame!

4 Hark, those bursts of acclamation!
Hark, those loud triumphant chords!
Jesus takes the highest station;
O what joy the sight affords!
  Crown Him! Crown Him!
King of kings, and Lord of lords!

362

1 Glory be to God the Father!
Glory be to God the Son!
Glory be to God the Spirit!
Great Jehovah, Three in one:
  Glory, glory,
While eternal ages run!

2 Glory be to Him who loved us,
Washed us from each spot and stain;
Glory be to Him who bought us
Made us kings with Him to reign:
  Glory, glory,
To the Lamb that once was slain!

3 Glory to the King of angels!
Glory to the church's King!
Glory to the King of nations!
Heaven and earth your praises bring:
  Glory, glory,
To the King of glory bring.

4 Glory, blessing, praise eternal!
Thus the choir of angels sings;
Honor, riches, power, dominion!
Thus its praise creation brings:
  Glory, glory,
Glory to the King of kings!

363

1 Angels, from the realms of glory,
Wing your flight o'er all the earth,
Ye who sang creation's story,
Now proclaim Messiah's birth;
  Come and worship,
Worship Christ, the new-born King.

2 Shepherds in the field abiding,
Watching o'er your flocks by night,
God with man is now residing;
Yonder shines the infant-light;
  Come and worship,
Worship Christ the new-born King.

3 Saints, before the altar bending,
Watching long in hope and fear,
Suddenly the Lord descending,
In His temple shall appear;
  Come and worship,
Worship Christ the new-born King.

364

1 O'er the gloomy hills of darkness,
Cheered by no celestial ray,
Sun of Righteousness arising,
Bring the bright, the glorious day;
  Send the Gospel
To the earth's remotest bound.

2 Kingdoms wide that sit in darkness,
Grant them, Lord, the glorious light,
And from eastern coast to western,
May the morning chase the night;
  And redemption,
Freely purchased, win the day!

3 Fly abroad, thou mighty Gospel,
Win and conquer, never cease;
May thy lasting, wide dominion
Multiply and still increase;
  Sway Thy sceptre,
Saviour, all the world around!

365

1 On the mountain's top appearing,
Lo! the sacred herald stands,
Welcome news to Zion bearing,
Zion, long in hostile lands:
   Mourning captive!
God Himself will loose thy bands.

2 Has thy night been long and mournful?
Have thy friends unfaithful proved?
Have thy foes been proud and scornful,
By thy sighs and tears unmoved?
   Cease thy mourning;
Zion still is well beloved.

3 God, thy God, will now restore thee;
He Himself appears thy friend;
All thy foes shall flee before thee;
Here their boasts and triumphs end:
   Great deliverance
Zion's King vouchsafes to send.

4 Enemies no more shall trouble;
All thy wrongs shall be redrest;
For thy shame thou shalt have double,
In thy Maker's favor blest;
   All thy conflicts
End in everlasting rest!

366

1 Yes, we trust the day is breaking;
Joyful times are near at hand;
God, the mighty God, is speaking
By His word in every land:
   When He chooses,
Darkness flies at His command.

2 Let us hail the joyful season;
Let us hail the dawning ray;
When the Lord appears there's reason
To expect a glorious day:
   At His presence
Gloom and darkness flee away.

3 While the foe becomes more daring,
While he enters like a flood,
God, the Saviour, is preparing
Means to spread His truth abroad;
   Every language
Soon shall tell the love of God.

4 God of Jacob, high and glorious,
Let Thy people see Thy hand!
Let the Gospel be victorious
Through the world in every land;
   And the idols
Perish, Lord, at Thy command!

367

1 Welcome, welcome, dear Redeemer,
Welcome to this heart of mine;
Lord, I make a full surrender,
Every power and thought be Thine;
   Thine entirely,
Through eternal ages Thine.

2 Known to all to be Thy mansion,
Earth and hell will disappear;
Or in vain attempt possession,
When they find the Lord is near.
   Shout, O Zion!
Shout, ye saints, the Lord is here!

368

1 Jesus comes to souls rejoicing,
Bringing news of sin forgiven;
Jesus comes in sounds of gladness,
Lifting up our souls to heaven;
   Hallelujah!
Now the gate of death is riven.

2 Jesus comes in joy and sorrow,
Shares alike our hopes and fears;
Jesus comes whate'er befalls us,
Glads our hearts and dries our tears,
   Hallelujah!
Cheering e'en our failing years.

3 Jesus comes on clouds, triumphant,
When the heavens shall pass away;
Jesus comes again in glory;
Let us then our homage pay:
   Hallelujah!
Sing we "till the break of day."

369

1 Lo! He comes, with clouds descending,
Once for favored sinners slain;
Thousand thousand saints attending
Swell the triumph of His train:
  Hallelujah!
Jesus comes, He comes to reign.

2 Every eye shall now behold Him,
Robed in dreadful majesty;
Those who set at naught, and sold Him,
Pierced and nailed Him to the tree,
  Deeply wailing,
Shall the true Messiah see.

3 Every island, sea, and mountain,
Heaven and earth, shall flee away;
All who hate Him must, confounded,
Hear the trump proclaim the day:
  Come to judgment!
Come to judgment! come away!

4 Yea, amen! let all adore Thee,
High on Thine eternal throne!
Saviour, take the power and glory,
Claim the kingdom for Thine own!
  O come quickly!
Hallelujah! come, Lord, come!

370

1 O'er the distant mountains breaking,
Comes the reddening dawn of day;
Rise, my soul, from sleep awaking,
Rise, and sing, and watch, and pray:
  'Tis thy Saviour,
On His bright, returning way.

2 O Thou long-expected, weary
Waits my anxious soul for Thee;
Life is dark, and earth is dreary,
Where Thy light I do not see:
  O my Saviour,
When wilt Thou return to me!

3 Long, too long, in sin and sadness,
Far away from Thee I pine;
When, O when shall I the gladness
Of Thy Spirit feel in mine!
  O my Saviour,
When shall I be wholly Thine!

4 Nearer is my soul's salvation,
Spent the night, the day at hand;
Keep me in my lowly station,
Watching for Thee, till I stand,
  O my Saviour,
In Thy bright and promised land!

371

1 Lo! He cometh, countless trumpets
Wake to life the slumbering dead;
'Mid ten thousand saints and angels
See their great exalted Head.
  Hallelujah!
Welcome, welcome, Son of God.

2 Full of joyful expectation,
Saints behold the Judge appear;
Truth and justice go before Him,
Now the joyful sentence hear;
  Hallelujah!
Welcome, welcome, Judge divine!

3 "Come, ye blessèd of my Father!
Enter into life and joy;
Banish all your fears and sorrows;
Endless praise be your employ;
  Hallelujah!
Welcome, welcome to the skies."

372

1 Hark! the voice of love and mercy
Sounds aloud from Calvary;
See! it rends the rocks asunder,
Shakes the earth, and veils the sky:
  "It is finished!"
Hear the dying Saviour cry.

2 "It is finished!"—O what pleasure
Do these precious words afford!
Heavenly blessings, without measure,
Flow to us from Christ the Lord:
  "It is finished!"
Saints, the dying words record.

3 Tune your harps anew, ye seraphs,
Join to sing the pleasing theme;
All on earth and all in heaven,
Join to praise Immanuel's name!
  Hallelujah!
Glory to the bleeding Lamb!

373

1 O my soul, what means this sadness!
Wherefore art thou thus cast down!
Let thy grief be turned to gladness;
Bid thy restless fears begone;
   Look to Jesus,
And rejoice in His dear name.

2 What though Satan's strong temptations
Vex and grieve thee day by day,
And thy sinful inclinations
Often fill thee with dismay;
   Thou shalt conquer
Through the Lamb's redeeming blood.

3 Though ten thousand ills beset thee
From without and from within,
Jesus saith He'll ne'er forget thee,
But will save from hell and sin;
   He is faithful
To perform His gracious word.

4 Though distresses now attend thee,
And thou tread'st the thorny road,
His right hand shall still defend thee;
Soon He'll bring thee home to God;
   Therefore praise Him,
Praise the great Redeemer's name.

374

1 Saviour, visit Thy plantation,
Grant us, Lord, a gracious rain!
All will come to desolation,
Unless Thou return again;
   Lord, revive us,
All our help must come from Thee!

2 Keep no longer at a distance,
Shine upon us from on high,
Lest for want of Thine assistance,
Every plant should droop and die.

3 Dearest Saviour, hasten hither,
Thou canst make them bloom again!
O permit them not to wither,
Let not all our hopes be vain.

4 Break the tempter's fatal power;
Turn the stony heart to flesh;
And begin from this good hour
To revive Thy work afresh.

375

1 Guide me, O Thou great Jehovah,
Pilgrim through this barren land;
I am weak, but Thou art mighty;
Hold me with Thy powerful hand;
   Bread of heaven!
Feed me till I want no more.

2 Open now the crystal fountain
Whence the healing streams do flow;
Let the fiery, cloudy pillar
Lead me all my journey through;
   Strong Deliverer!
Be Thou still my strength and shield.

3 When I tread the verge of Jordan,
Bid my anxious fears subside;
Death of death, and hell's destruction,
Land me safe on Canaan's side;
   Songs of praises
I will ever give to Thee.

376

1 Lord, dismiss us with Thy blessing;
Fill our hearts with joy and peace;
Let us now, Thy love possessing,
Triumph in redeeming grace:
   O refresh us,
Travelling through this wilderness.

2 Thanks we give, and adoration,
For Thy gospel's joyful sound;
May the fruits of Thy salvation
In our hearts and lives abound;
   May Thy presence
With us evermore be found.

3 So, whene'er the signal's given
Us from earth to call away,
Borne on angels' wings to heaven,
Glad the summons to obey,
   May we ever
Reign with Christ in endless day!

86 CHRISTIAN PRAISE.

CHRISTMAS HYMN. H. M.

DARWELL'S. H. M.

377

1 Rejoice! the Lord is King,
Your Lord and King adore;
Mortals, give thanks and sing,
And triumph evermore :
Lift up your heart, lift up your voice;
Rejoice! again I say, Rejoice!

2 Jesus the Saviour reigns,
The God of truth and love;
When He had purged our stains,
He took His seat above :
Lift up your heart, lift up your voice;
Rejoice! again I say, Rejoice!

3 He all His foes shall quell,
Shall all our sins destroy,
And every bosom swell
With pure seraphic joy :
Lift up your heart, lift up your voice;
Rejoice! again I say, Rejoice!

4 Rejoice in glorious hope;
Jesus, the Judge, shall come,
And take His servants up
To their eternal home :
We soon shall hear the archangel's voice;
The trump of God shall sound, Rejoice!

378

1 O Zion, tune thy voice,
And raise thy hands on high;
Tell all the earth thy joys,
And boast salvation nigh :
Cheerful in God, arise and shine,
While rays divine stream all abroad.

2 In honor to His name,
Reflect that sacred light,
And loud that grace proclaim
Which makes thy darkness bright:
Pursue His praise till sovereign love
In worlds above thy glory raise.

3 There, on His holy hill,
A brighter sun shall rise,
And with His radiance fill
Those fairer, purer skies :
While round His throne ten thousand stars
In nobler spheres His influence own.

379

1 Hark! hark! the notes of joy
Roll o'er the heavenly plains,
And seraphs find employ
For their sublimest strains;
Some new delight in heaven is known;
Loud sound the harps around the throne.

2 Hark! hark! the sounds draw nigh,
The joyful hosts descend;
Jesus forsakes the sky,
To earth His footsteps bend;
He comes to bless our fallen race;
He comes with messages of grace.

3 Strike, strike the harps again,
To great Immanuel's name;
Arise, ye sons of men,
And all His grace proclaim;
Angels and men, wake every string,
'Tis God the Saviour's praise we sing!

380

1 We give immortal praise
For God the Father's love,
For all our comforts here,
And better hopes above;
He sent His own eternal Son
To die for sins that we had done.

2 To God the Son belongs
Immortal glory too;
Who bought us with His blood
From everlasting woe :
And now He lives and now He reigns,
And sees the fruit of all His pains.

3 To God the Spirit's name
Immortal worship give,
Whose new-creating power
Makes the dead sinner live :
His work completes the great design,
And fills the soul with joy divine.

4 Almighty God, to Thee
Be endless honors done,
The undivided Three,
The great and glorious One :
Where reason fails with all her powers,
There faith prevails and love adores.

381

1 Come, every pious heart
  That loves the Saviour's name,
  Your noblest power exert
  To celebrate His fame:
  Tell all above and all below,
  The debt of love to Him you owe.

2 He left His starry crown,
  And laid His robes aside;
  On wings of love came down,
  And wept, and bled, and died:
  What He endured, O who can tell,
  To save our souls from death and hell!

3 From the dark grave He rose,
  The mansion of the dead;
  And thence His mighty foes
  In glorious triumph led:
  Up through the sky the Conqueror rode,
  And reigns on high, the Saviour, God.

4 From thence He'll quickly come,
  His chariot will not stay,
  And bear our spirits home
  To realms of endless day:
  There shall we see His lovely face,
  And ever be in His embrace.

382

1 Welcome, delightful morn,
  Thou day of sacred rest;
  I hail thy kind return;
  Lord, make these moments blest!
  From the low train of mortal toys
  I soar to reach immortal joys.

2 Now may the King descend
  And fill His throne of grace;
  Thy sceptre, Lord, extend,
  While saints address Thy face;
  Let sinners feel Thy quickening word,
  And learn to know and fear the Lord.

3 Descend, celestial Dove,
  With all Thy quickening powers;
  Disclose a Saviour's love,
  And bless the sacred hours:
  Then shall my soul new life obtain,
  Nor Sabbaths be indulged in vain.

383

1 Join all the glorious names
  Of wisdom, love, and power,
  That ever mortals knew,
  That angels ever bore—
  All are too mean to speak His worth,
  Too mean to set my Saviour forth.

2 Great Prophet of my God,
  My tongue would bless Thy name;
  By Thee the joyful news
  Of our salvation came:
  The joyful news of sins forgiven,
  Of hell subdued, and peace with heaven.

3 Jesus, my great High-priest,
  Offered His blood and died;
  My guilty conscience seeks
  No sacrifice beside:
  His powerful blood did once atone,
  And now it pleads before the throne.

4 My dear Almighty Lord,
  My Conqueror and my King!
  Thy sceptre and Thy sword,
  Thy reigning grace I sing:
  Thine is the power; behold, I sit
  In willing bonds beneath Thy feet.

384

1 Awake, ye saints, awake!
  And hail this sacred day;
  In loftiest songs of praise
  Your joyful homage pay;
  Come, bless the day that God hath blest,
  The type of heaven's eternal rest.

2 On this auspicious morn
  The Lord of life arose,
  And burst the bars of death,
  And vanquished all our foes:
  And now He pleads our cause above,
  And reaps the fruit of all His love.

3 All hail, triumphant Lord!
  Heaven with hosannas rings;
  And earth, in humbler strains,
  Thy praise responsive sings:
  "Worthy the Lamb that once was slain,
  Through endless years to live and reign!"

385

1 Blow ye the trumpet, blow!
  The gladly solemn sound
  Let all the nations know,
  To earth's remotest bound!
  The year of jubilee is come;
  Return, ye ransomed sinners, home.

2 Jesus, our great High-priest,
  Has full atonement made;
  Ye weary spirits, rest;
  Ye mournful souls, be glad.

3 Extol the Lamb of God,
  The sin-atoning Lamb!
  Redemption by His blood,
  Through every land, proclaim.

4 Ye who have sold for naught
  Your heritage above,
  Receive it back unbought,
  The gift of Jesus' love.

5 Ye slaves of sin and hell,
  Your liberty receive,
  And safe in Jesus dwell,
  And blest in Jesus live.

386

1 To your Creator, God,
  Your great preserver, raise,
  Ye creatures of His hand,
  Your highest notes of praise:
  Let every voice proclaim His power,
  His name adore, and loud rejoice.

2 Let every creature join
  To celebrate His Name,
  And all their various powers
  Assist the exalted theme:
  Let nature raise, from every tongue,
  A general song of grateful praise.

3 But O from human tongues
  Should nobler praises flow;
  And every thankful heart
  With warm devotion glow;
  Your voices raise above the rest;
  Ye highly blest, declare His praise.

4 Assist me, gracious God!
  My heart, my voice inspire;
  Then shall I grateful join
  The universal choir.
  Thy grace can raise my heart, my tongue,
  And tune my song to lively praise.

387

1 Yes, the Redeemer rose,
  The Saviour left the dead,
  And o'er our hellish foes
  High raised His conquering head;
  In wild dismay, the guards around
  Fall to the ground and sink away.

2 To heaven the angels fly,
  The joyful news to bear;
  Hark! as they soar on high,
  What music fills the air!
  Their anthems say, "Jesus who bled
  Hath left the dead; He rose to-day."

3 Ye mortals, catch the sound,
  Redeemed by Him from hell,
  And send the echo round
  The globe on which you dwell;
  Transported cry, "Jesus who bled
  Hath left the dead, no more to die."

4 All hail, triumphant Lord,
  Who sav'st us with Thy blood!
  Wide be Thy Name adored,
  Thou rising, reigning God!
  With Thee we rise, with Thee we reign,
  And empires gain beyond the skies.

388

1 God is gone up on high
  With a triumphant noise;
  The clarions of the sky
  Proclaim the angelic joys:
  Join, all on earth, rejoice and sing,
  Glory ascribe to glory's King.

2 All power to our great Lord
  Is by the Father given;
  By angel hosts adored,
  He reigns supreme in heaven.

3 High on His holy seat,
  He bears the righteous sway;
  His foes beneath His feet
  Shall sink and die away.

4 Then shall the earth, renewed
  In righteousness divine,
  With all the hosts of God,
  In one great chorus join.

389
Psalm 121.

1 Upward I lift mine eyes;
 From God is all my aid;
 The God who built the skies,
 And earth and nature made:
God is the tower to which I fly;
His grace is nigh in every hour.

2 My feet shall never slide
 And fall in fatal snares,
 Since God, my guard and guide,
 Defends me from my fears:
Those wakeful eyes that never sleep,
Shall Israel keep when dangers rise.

3 No burning heats by day,
 Nor blasts of evening air,
 Shall take my health away,
 If God be with me there:
Thou art my sun, and Thou my shade,
To guard my head by night or noon.

4 Hast Thou not given Thy word
 To save my soul from death!
 And I can trust my Lord
 To keep my mortal breath:
I'll go and come, nor fear to die,
Till from on high Thou call me home.

390
Psalm 93.

1 The Lord Jehovah reigns;
 His throne is built on high;
 The garments He assumes
 Are light and majesty;
His glories shine with beams so bright
No mortal eye can bear the sight.

2 The thunders of His hand
 Keep the wide world in awe;
 His wrath and justice stand
 To guard His holy law;
And where His love resolves to bless,
His truth confirms and seals the grace.

3 And can this mighty King
 Of glory condescend,
 And will He write His name,
 My Father and my Friend!
I love His name, I love His word;
Join all my powers, and praise the Lord!

391
Psalm 84.

1 Lord of the worlds above,
 How pleasant and how fair
 The dwellings of Thy love,
 Thine earthly temples are!
To Thine abode my heart aspires,
With warm desires to see my God.

2 O happy souls that pray
 Where God appoints to hear!
 O happy men that pay
 Their constant service there!
They praise Thee still, and happy they
That love the way to Zion's hill.

3 They go from strength to strength,
 Through this dark vale of tears;
 Till each arrives at length,
 Till each in heaven appears:
O glorious seat, when God our King
Shall thither bring our willing feet!

392
Psalm 18.

1 The Lord Jehovah lives,
 And blessèd be my rock!
 Though earth her bosom heaves
 And mountains feel the shock,
Though oceans rage and torrents roar,
He is the same for evermore.

2 The Lord Jehovah lives,
 The dying sinner's Friend;
 How freely He forgives
 The follies that offend!
He wipes the penitential tear,
Bids faith and hope the spirit cheer.

3 The Lord Jehovah lives
 To hear and answer prayer;
 Whoe'er in Him believes
 And trusts His guardian care,
A Father's tender love shall know,
Whence living streams of comfort flow.

4 The Lord Jehovah lives
 Salvation to secure;
 The title that He gives
 Will be forever sure;
'Tis drawn in characters of blood,
'Tis issued from the throne of God.

393

1 Stand up, stand up for Jesus,
  Ye soldiers of the cross!
  Lift high His royal banner,
  It must not suffer loss:
  From victory unto victory
  His army shall He lead,
  Till every foe is vanquished,
  And Christ is Lord indeed.

2 Stand up, stand up for Jesus!
  Stand in His strength alone;
  The arm of flesh will fail you,
  Ye dare not trust your own:
  Put on the gospel armor,
  And watching unto prayer,
  Where duty calls or danger,
  Be never wanting there.

3 Stand up, stand up for Jesus!
  The strife will not be long;
  This day the noise of battle,
  The next the victor's song:
  To him that overcometh,
  A crown of life shall be;
  He with the King of Glory
  Shall reign eternally.

394

1 Now be the gospel banner
  In every land unfurled;
  And be the shout—"Hosanna!"
  Reëchoed through the world;
  Till every isle and nation,
  Till every tribe and tongue
  Receive the great salvation,
  And join the happy throng.

2 What though th' embattled legions
  Of earth and hell combine!
  His arm, throughout their regions,
  Shall soon resplendent shine:
  Ride on, O Lord, victorious,
  Immanuel, Prince of peace!
  Thy triumph shall be glorious,
  Thy empire still increase.

3 Yes, Thou shalt reign forever,
  O Jesus, King of kings!
  Thy light, Thy love, Thy favor,
  Each ransomed captive sings:
  The isles for Thee are waiting,
  The deserts learn Thy praise,
  The hills and valleys greeting,
  The song responsive raise.

395

1 O day of rest and gladness,
  O day of joy and light,
  O balm of care and sadness,
  Most beautiful, most bright;
  On thee, the high and lowly,
  Through ages joined in tune,
  Sing, "Holy, holy, holy,"
  To the Great God Triune.

2 On thee, at the creation,
  The light first had its birth;
  On thee, for our salvation
  Christ rose from depths of earth;
  On thee, our Lord victorious,
  The Spirit sent from heaven,
  And thus on thee, most glorious,
  A triple light was given.

3 May we, new graces gaining
  From this our day of rest,
  Attain the rest remaining
  To spirits of the blest;
  And there, our voice upraising
  To Father and to Son,
  And Holy Ghost, be praising
  Ever the Three in One.

396

1 When shall the voice of singing
  Flow joyfully along?
  When hill and valley ringing
  With one triumphant song,
  Proclaim the contest ended,
  And Him who once was slain,
  Again to earth descended,
  In righteousness to reign!

2 Then from the craggy mountains
  The sacred shout shall fly;
  And shady vales and fountains
  Shall echo the reply:
  High tower and lowly dwelling
  Shall send the chorus round,
  All hallelujah swelling
  In one eternal sound.

397

1. Jerusalem the golden
With milk and honey blest!
Beneath thy contemplation
Sink heart and voice opprest;
I know not, O I know not
What social joys are there;
What radiancy of glory,
What light beyond compare.

2. They stand, those halls of Zion,
Conjubilant with song,
And bright with many an angel,
And all the martyr throng.
The Prince is ever in them;
The daylight is serene;
The pastures of the blessèd
Are decked in glorious sheen.

3. There is the throne of David;
And there, from care released,
The song of them that triumph,
The shout of them that feast;
And they who with their Leader
Have conquered in the fight,
Forever and forever
Are clad in robes of white.

398

1. From every earthly pleasure,
From every transient joy,
From every mortal treasure
That soon will fade and die;
No longer these desiring,
Upward our wishes tend,
To nobler bliss aspiring,
And joys that never end.

2. From every piercing sorrow
That heaves our breast to-day,
Or threatens us to-morrow,
Hope turns our eyes away;
On wings of faith ascending,
We see the land of light,
And feel our sorrows ending,
In infinite delight.

3. 'Tis true we are but strangers
And pilgrims here below,
And countless snares and dangers
Surround the path we go;
Though painful and distressing,
Yet there's a rest above;
And onward still we're pressing,
To reach that land of love.

399

1. Jerusalem the glorious!
The glory of the elect!
O dear and future vision
That eager hearts expect!

2. For thee, O dear, dear country,
Mine eyes their vigils keep;
For very love, beholding
Thy happy name, they weep.

3. O sweet and blessèd country,
Shall I e'er win thy grace?
O sweet and blessèd country,
Shall I e'er see thy face?

4. O one, O only mansion,
O paradise of joy,
Where tears are ever banished,
And smiles have no alloy!

5. Thy ageless walls are bonded
With amethyst unpriced;
Thy saints build up its fabric,
The corner-stone is Christ.

6. The cross is all thy splendor,
The Crucified thy praise;
His laud and benediction
Thy ransomed people raise.

400

1. To Thee, my God and Saviour,
My heart exulting springs,
Rejoicing in Thy favor,
Almighty King of kings.
I'll celebrate Thy glory,
With all the saints above,
And tell the wondrous story
Of Thy redeeming love.

2. By Thee through life supported,
I pass the dangerous road,
With heavenly hosts escorted
Up to their bright abode;
There cast my crown before Thee,
My toils and conflicts o'er,
And day and night adore Thee:
What can an angel more!

401

1 From Greenland's icy mountains,
  From India's coral strand,
  Where Afric's sunny fountains
  Roll down their golden sand,
  From many an ancient river,
  From many a palmy plain,
  They call us to deliver
  Their land from error's chain.

2 What though the spicy breezes
  Blow soft o'er Céylon's isle;
  Though every prospect pleases,
  And only man is vile!
  In vain with lavish kindness
  The gifts of God are strown;
  The heathen, in his blindness,
  Bows down to wood and stone.

3 Can we, whose souls are lighted
  With wisdom from on high—
  Can we to men benighted
  The lamp of life deny!
  Salvation, O salvation,
  The joyful sound proclaim,
  Till each remotest nation
  Has learned Messiah's name.

4 Waft, waft, ye winds, His story,
  And you, ye waters, roll,
  Till like a sea of glory
  It spreads from pole to pole;
  Till o'er our ransomed nature
  The Lamb for sinners slain,
  Redeemer, King, Creator,
  In bliss returns to reign!

402

1 Rejoice, all ye believers,
  And let your lights appear;
  The evening is advancing,
  And darker night is near;
  The Bridegroom is arising,
  And soon He draweth nigh;
  Up! pray, and watch, and wrestle!
  At midnight comes the cry.

2 Our Hope and Expectation,
  O Jesus, now appear;
  Arise, Thou Son so longed for,
  O'er this benighted sphere!
  With heart and hands uplifted,
  We plead, O Lord, to see
  The day of earth's redemption,
  That brings us unto Thee!

403   Psalm 72.

1 Hail to the Lord's Anointed,
  Great David's greater Son!
  Hail, in the time appointed
  His reign on earth begun!
  He comes to break oppression,
  To set the captive free,
  To take away transgression,
  And rule in equity.

2 He comes with succor speedy
  To those who suffer wrong;
  To help the poor and needy,
  And bid the weak be strong;
  To give them songs for sighing,
  Their darkness turn to light,
  Whose souls, condemned and dying,
  Were precious in His sight.

3 He shall come down like showers
  Upon the fruitful earth,
  And love and joy, like flowers,
  Spring in His path to birth.
  Before Him on the mountains
  Shall peace, the herald, go;
  And righteousness in fountains
  From hill to valley flow.

4 For Him shall prayer unceasing
  And daily vows ascend;
  His kingdom still increasing,
  A kingdom without end;
  The tide of time shall never
  His covénant remove;
  His name shall stand forever,
  That name to us is Love.

404

1 O SACRED Head, now wounded,
With grief and shame weighed down,
Now scornfully surrounded
With thorns, Thine only crown;
O sacred Head, what glory,
What bliss, till now was Thine!
Yet though despised and gory,
I joy to call Thee mine.

2 What language shall I borrow
To thank Thee, dearest Friend,
For this Thy dying sorrow,
Thy pity without end!
O make me Thine forever;
And should I fainting be,
Lord, let me never, never,
Outlive my love to Thee!

3 Be near me when I'm dying,
O show Thy cross to me!
And for my succor flying,
Come, Lord, and set me free!
These eyes, new faith receiving,
From Jesus shall not move;
For he who dies believing,
Dies safely, through Thy love.

405

1 O BREAD to pilgrims given,
O Food that angels eat,
O Manna sent from heaven,
For heaven-born natures meet!
Give us, for Thee long pining,
To eat till richly filled;
Till, earth's delight resigning,
Our every wish is stilled!

2 O Water life bestowing,
From out the Saviour's heart!
A fountain purely flowing,
A fount of love Thou art.
O let us, freely tasting,
Our burning thirst assuage!
Thy sweetness, never wasting,
Avails from age to age.

3 Jesus, this feast receiving,
We Thee unseen adore;
Thy faithful word believing,
We take, and doubt no more:
Give us, Thou true and loving,
On earth to live in Thee;
Then, death the veil removing,
Thy glorious face to see!

406

1 LORD JESUS, by Thy Passion
To Thee I make my prayer;
Thou who in mercy smitest,
Have mercy, Lord, and spare.
O wash me in the fountain
That floweth from Thy side;
O clothe me in the raiment
Thy Blood hath purified.

2 O hold Thou up my goings,
And lead from strength to strength,
That unto Thee in Zion
I may appear at length.
O make my spirit worthy
To join that ransomed throng;
O teach my lips to utter
That everlasting song.

3 O give that last, best blessing
That even saints can know:
To follow in Thy footsteps
Wherever Thou dost go.
Not wisdom, might, or glory,
I ask to win above;
I ask for Thee, Thee only,
O Thou Eternal Love!

407

1 I KNOW no life divided,
O Lord of life, from Thee;
In Thee is life provided
For all mankind, for me:
I know no death, O Jesus,
Because I live in Thee;
Thy death it is which frees us
From death eternally.

2 I fear no tribulation,
Since, whatsoe'er it be,
It makes no separation
Between my Lord and me.
If Thou, my God, my Teacher,
Vouchsafe to be my own,
Though poor, I shall be richer
Than monarch on his throne.

408

1 Rise, my soul, and stretch thy wings,
Thy better portion trace;
Rise from transitory things
Towards heaven, thy native place.
Sun and moon and stars decay;
Time shall soon this earth remove;
Rise, my soul, and haste away
To seats prepared above.

2 Rivers to the ocean run,
Nor stay in all their course;
Fire, ascending, seeks the sun;
Both speed them to their source;
So a soul that's born of God,
Pants to view His glorious face,
Upward tends to His abode,
To rest in His embrace.

3 Fly me, riches, fly me, cares,
Whilst I that coast explore;
Flattering world, with all thy snares,
Solicit me no more!
Pilgrims fix not here their home;
Strangers tarry but a night;
When the last dear morn is come,
They'll rise to joyful light.

4 Cease, ye pilgrims, cease to mourn,
Press onward to the prize;
Soon our Saviour will return,
Triumphant in the skies:
Yet a season, and you know
Happy entrance will be given,
All our sorrows left below,
And earth exchanged for heaven.

409 [Leconey.]

1 Lamb of God, whose bleeding love
We now recall to mind,
Send the answer from above,
And let us mercy find.
Think on us who think on Thee;
Every burdened soul release;
O remember Calvary,
And bid us go in peace!

2 By thine agonizing pain,
And bloody sweat, we pray,
By thy dying love to man,
Take all our sins away.
Burst our bonds and set us free,
From our crime and guilt release;
O remember Calvary,
And bid us go in peace!

3 Let Thy blood, by faith applied,
The sinner's pardon seal;
Speak us freely justified,
And all our sickness heal;
By Thy passion on the tree,
Let our griefs and troubles cease.
O remember Calvary,
And bid us go in peace.

4 Can we ever hence depart
Till Thou our wants relieve!
Write forgiveness on our heart,
And all Thine image give.
Still our souls shall cry to Thee,
Till renewed by holiness.
O remember Calvary,
And bid us go in peace.

410 [Leconey.]

1 Time is winging us away
To our eternal home;
Life is but a winter's day,
A journey to the tomb;
Youth and vigor soon will flee,
Blooming beauty lose its charms;
All that's mortal soon will be
Enclosed in death's cold arms.

2 Time is winging us away
To our eternal home;
Life is but a winter's day,
A journey to the tomb;
But the Christian shall enjoy
Health and beauty soon above;
Far beyond the world's alloy,
Secure in Jesus' love.

411

1 I lay my sins on Jesus,
  The spotless Lamb of God;
  He bears them all, and frees us
  From the accursèd load.
  I bring my guilt to Jesus,
  To wash my crimson stains
  White in His blood most precious,
  Till not a spot remains.

2 I lay my wants on Jesus;
  All fulness dwells in Him;
  He heals all my diseases,
  He doth my soul redeem.
  I lay my griefs on Jesus,
  My burdens and my cares;
  He from them all releases,
  He all my sorrows shares.

3 I rest my soul on Jesus,
  This weary soul of mine;
  His right hand me embraces,
  I on His breast recline.
  I love the name of Jesus,
  Immanuel, Christ, the Lord;
  Like fragrance on the breezes
  His name abroad is poured.

412

1 Lord of the vast creation,
  Support of worlds unknown,
  Desire of every nation!
  Behold us at Thy throne;
  We come for mercy crying,
  Through Thine atoning blood;
  And on Thy grace relying,
  We seek each promised good.

2 We bless the condescension
  That brought Thee down to earth;
  Of which the seers made mention,
  Who prophesied Thy birth.
  We celebrate the glory
  That marked Thy wondrous way,
  And own the joyful story
  That claims this hallowed day.

3 O when shall Thy salvation
  Be known through every land,
  And men, in every station,
  Obey Thy great command!
  In God's own Son believing,
  From sin may they be free;
  And gospel-grace receiving,
  Find life and peace in Thee.

413

1 Sometimes a light surprises
  The Christian while he sings;
  It is the Lord who rises
  With healing in His wings.
  When comforts are declining,
  He grants the soul again
  A season of clear shining,
  To cheer it after rain.

2 In holy contemplation,
  We sweetly then pursue
  The theme of God's salvation,
  And find it ever new.
  Set free from present sorrow,
  We cheerfully can say,
  Let the unknown to-morrow
  Bring with it what it may,

3 It can bring with it nothing,
  But He will bear us through;
  Who gives the lilies clothing
  Will clothe His people too.
  Beneath the spreading heavens,
  No creature but is fed,
  And He who feeds the ravens
  Will give His children bread.

4 Though vine nor fig-tree neither
  Their wonted fruit should bear,
  Though all the fields should wither
  Nor flocks nor herds be there,
  Yet God the same abiding,
  His praise shall tune my voice,
  For while in Him confiding,
  I cannot but rejoice.

414

1 Come, Thou Almighty King,
　Help us Thy name to sing,
　　Help us to praise:
　Father all-glorious,
　O'er all victorious,
　Come, and reign over us,
　　Ancient of Days!

2 Come, Thou Incarnate Word,
　Gird on Thy mighty sword;
　　Our prayer attend!
　Come, and Thy people bless,
　And give Thy word success:
　Spirit of holiness,
　　On us descend!

3 Come, Holy Comforter,
　Thy sacred witness bear,
　　In this glad hour!
　Thou, who almighty art,
　Now rule in every heart,
　And ne'er from us depart,
　　Spirit of power!

4 To the great One in Three
　The highest praises be,
　　Hence evermore!
　His sovereign majesty
　May we in glory see,
　And to eternity
　　Love and adore.

415

1 Rise, glorious Conqueror, rise
　Into Thy native skies;
　　Assume Thy right;
　And where in many a fold
　The clouds are backward rolled,
　Pass through those gates of gold,
　　And reign in light!

2 Victor o'er death and hell,
　Cherubic legions swell
　　Thy radiant train;
　Praises all heaven inspire,
　Each angel sweeps his lyre,
　And waves his wings of fire,
　　Thou Lamb once slain!

3 Enter, Incarnate God!
　No feet but Thine have trod
　　The serpent down;
　Blow the full trumpets, blow!
　Wider yon portals throw!
　Saviour, triumphant, go
　　And take Thy crown!

416

1 Glory to God on high!
　Let heaven and earth reply,
　　Praise ye His name!
　His love and grace adore,
　Who all our sorrows bore
　And sing for evermore:
　　Worthy the Lamb!

2 All they around the throne,
　Cheerfully join in one,
　　Praising His name:
　We, who have felt His blood
　Sealing our peace with God,
　Sound His dear name abroad:
　　Worthy the Lamb!

3 Join, all ye ransomed race,
　Our Lord and God to bless;
　　Praise ye His name.
　In Him we will rejoice,
　And make a joyful noise,
　Shouting with heart and voice:
　　Worthy the Lamb!

417 *Psalm 150.*

1 Praise ye Jehovah's name,
　Praise through His courts proclaim,
　　Rise and adore:
　High o'er the heavens above,
　Sound His great acts of love,
　While His rich grace we prove
　　Vast as His power.

2 Now let the trumpet raise
　Sounds of triumphant praise,
　　Wide as His fame.
　There let the harp be found;
　Organs, with solemn sound,
　Roll your deep notes around,
　　Filled with His name.

3 While His high praise ye sing,
　Shake every sounding string;
　　Sweet the accord!
　He vital breath bestows;
　Let every breath that flows
　His noblest fame disclose;
　　Praise ye the Lord!

418

1 My faith looks up to Thee
Thou Lamb of Calvary,
  Saviour Divine!
Now hear me while I pray,
Take all my guilt away,
O let me from this day
  Be wholly Thine.

2 May Thy rich grace impart
Strength to my fainting heart,
  My zeal inspire;
As Thou hast died for me,
O may my love to Thee
Pure, warm, and changeless be,
  A living fire.

3 While life's dark maze I tread,
And griefs around me spread,
  Be Thou my guide;
Bid darkness turn to day,
Wipe sorrow's tears away,
Nor let me ever stray
  From Thee aside.

When ends life's transient dream,
When death's cold, sullen stream
  Shall o'er me roll,
Blest Saviour, then, in love
Fear and distrust remove;
O bear me safe above,
  A ransomed soul.

419

1 Shepherd of tender youth,
Guiding in love and truth
  Through devious ways—
Christ, our triumphant King,
We come Thy name to sing,
And here our children bring,
  To shout Thy praise.

2 Thou art our only Lord,
O all-subduing Word,
  Healer of strife:
Thou didst Thyself abase,
That from sin's deep disgrace
Thou mightest save our race,
  And give us life.

3 Ever be near our side,
Our shepherd and our guide,
  Our staff and song;
Jesus, thou Christ of God,
By Thine enduring word
Lead us where Thou hast trod;
  Make our faith strong.

4 So now, and till we die,
Sound we Thy praises high,
  And joyful sing:
Babes and the gladsome throng,
Who to Thy church belong,
Unite to swell the song
  To Christ our King!

420

1 Nearer, my God, to Thee,
  Nearer to Thee!
Even though it be a cross
  That raiseth me,
Still all my song shall be:
Nearer, my God, to Thee,
  Nearer to Thee!

2 Though like the wanderer,
  The sun gone down,
Darkness be over me,
  My rest a stone;
Yet in my dreams I'd be
Nearer, my God, to Thee,
  Nearer to Thee!

3 There let the way appear
  Steps unto heaven;
All that Thou sendest me
  In mercy given;
Angels to beckon me
Nearer, my God, to Thee,
  Nearer to Thee!

4 Then with my waking thoughts
  Bright with Thy praise,
Out of my stony griefs
  Bethel I'll raise;
So by my woes to be
Nearer, my God, to Thee,
  Nearer to Thee

5 Or if on joyful wing
  Cleaving the sky,
Sun, moon, and stars forgot,
  Upward I fly;
Still all my song shall be,
Nearer, my God, to Thee,
  Nearer to Thee.

421

1 My country, 'tis of thee,
　Sweet land of liberty,
　　Of thee I sing:
　Land where my fathers died,
　Land of the pilgrims' pride,
　From every mountain side
　　Let freedom ring!

2 My native country, thee,
　Land of the noble free,
　　Thy name I love:
　I love thy rocks and rills,
　Thy woods and templed hills;
　My heart with rapture thrills
　　Like that above.

3 Let music swell the breeze,
　And ring from all the trees
　　Sweet freedom's song;
　Let mortal tongues awake,
　Let all that breathe partake,
　Let rocks their silence break,
　　The sound prolong.

4 Our fathers' God, to Thee,
　Author of liberty,
　　To Thee we sing;
　Long may our land be bright
　With freedom's holy light,
　Protect us by Thy might,
　　Great God, our King!

422

1 The God of harvest praise,
　In loud thanksgiving raise
　　Hand, heart, and voice!
　The valleys laugh and sing;
　Forests and mountains ring;
　The plains their tribute bring;
　　The streams rejoice.

2 Yea, bless His holy Name,
　And joyous thanks proclaim
　　Through all the earth;
　To glory in your lot
　Is comely, but be not
　God's benefits forgot
　　Amid your mirth.

3 The God of harvest praise,
　Hands, hearts, and voices raise,
　　With sweet accord;
　From field to garner throng,
　Bearing your sheaves along,
　And in your harvest song
　　Bless ye the Lord.

423

1 God bless our native land!
　Firm may she ever stand,
　　Through storm and night:
　When the wild tempests rave,
　Ruler of wind and wave,
　Do Thou our country save
　　By Thy great might!

2 For her our prayer shall rise
　To God, above the skies;
　　On Him we wait:
　Thou who art ever nigh,
　Guarding with watchful eye,
　To Thee aloud we cry,
　　God save the state!

424

1 Let us awake our joys;
　Strike up with cheerful voice;
　　Each creature, sing;
　Angels, begin the song;
　Mortals, the strain prolong,
　In accents sweet and strong,
　　"Jesus is King."

2 Proclaim abroad His name;
　Tell of His matchless fame,
　　What wonders done;
　Above, beneath, around,
　Let all the earth resound,
　Till heaven's high arch rebound,
　　"Victory is won."

3 He vanquished sin and hell,
　And our last foe will quell.
　　Mourners, rejoice,
　His dying love adore;
　Praise Him, now raised in power;
　Praise Him for evermore,
　　With joyful voice.

4 All hail the glorious day,
　When, through the heavenly way,
　　Lo! He shall come.
　While they who pierced Him wail,
　His promise shall not fail;
　Saints, see your King prevail:
　　Great Saviour, come!

425

1 Brightest and best of the sons of the morning,
   Dawn on our darkness, and lend us thine aid;
   Star of the East, the horizon adorning,
   Guide where our Infant Redeemer is laid!

2 Cold on His cradle the dew-drops are shining;
   Low lies His head with the beasts of the stall;
   Angels adore Him in slumber reclining,
   Maker, and Monarch, and Saviour of all!

3 Say shall we yield Him in costly devotion,
   Odors of Edom, and offerings divine!
   Gems of the mountain, and pearls of the ocean,
   Myrrh from the forest, or gold from the mine?

4 Vainly we offer each ample oblation;
   Vainly with gifts would His favor secure;
   Richer by far is the heart's adoration;
   Dearer to God are the prayers of the poor.

426

1 Ye angels, who stand round the throne,
   And view my Immanuel's face,
   In rapturous songs make Him known,
   Tune, tune your soft harps to His praise.

2 He formed you the spirits you are,
   So happy, so noble, so good;
   When others sunk down in despair,
   Confirmed by His power ye stood.

3 Ye saints, who stand nearer than they,
   And cast your bright crowns at His feet,
   His grace and His glory display,
   And all His rich mercy repeat.

4 He snatched you from hell and the grave,
   He ransomed from death and despair;
   For you He was mighty to save,
   Almighty to bring you safe there.

5 I want to put on my attire,
   Washed white in the blood of the Lamb;
   I want to be one of your choir,
   And tune my sweet harp to His name.

6 I want, O I want to be there,
   Where sorrow and sin bid adieu,
   Your joy and your friendship to share,
   To wonder and worship with you.

427

1 To Jesus, the crown of my hope,
   My soul is in haste to be gone;
   O bear me, ye cherubim, up
   And waft me away to His throne!

2 My Saviour whom absent I love,
   Whom not having seen I adore,
   Whose name is exalted above
   All glory, dominion, and power;

3 Dissolve Thou these bands that detain
   My soul from her portion in Thee;
   O strike off this adamant chain,
   And make me eternally free!

4 When that happy era begins,
   When arrayed in Thy glories I shine,
   Nor grieve any more by my sins
   The bosom on which I recline;

5 O then shall the veil be removed,
   And round me Thy brightness be poured;
   I shall meet Him whom absent I loved;
   I shall see Whom unseen I adored;

6 And then, never more shall the fears,
   The trials, temptations, and woes
   Which darken this valley of tears
   Intrude on my blissful repose.

428

1 Holy, holy, holy! Lord God Almighty!
Early in the morning our song shall rise to Thee:
Holy, holy, holy, merciful and mighty;
God in Three Persons, Blessed Trinity!

2 Holy, holy, holy! all the saints adore Thee,
Casting down their golden crowns around the glassy sea,
Cherubim and seraphim falling down before Thee,
Which wert, and art, and evermore shalt be.

3 Holy, holy, holy, though the darkness hide Thee,
Though the eye of sinful man Thy glory may not see,
Only Thou art holy; there is none beside Thee
Perfect in power, in love, and purity.

4 Holy, holy, holy! Lord God Almighty!
All Thy works shall praise Thy name, in earth, and sky, and sea;
Holy, holy, holy! merciful and mighty;
God in Three Persons, Blessed Trinity!

429   Psalm 48.

1 O GREAT is Jehovah, and great be His praise;
In the city of God He is King;
Proclaim ye His triumphs in jubilant lays;
On the mount of His holiness sing.

2 The joy of the earth, from her beautiful height,
Is Zion's impregnable hill;
The Lord in her temple still taketh delight;
God reigns in her palaces still.

3 Go, walk about Zion, and measure the length,
Her walls and her bulwarks, mark well;
Contemplate her palaces, glorious in strength,
Her towers and her pinnacles tell.

4 Then say to your children, "Our stronghold is tried;
This God is our God to the end;
His people forever His counsels shall guide,
His arm shall forever defend."

430   Psalm 100.

1 BE joyful in God, all ye lands of the earth;
O serve Him with gladness and fear;
Exult in His presence with music and mirth,
With love and devotion draw near.

2 Jehovah is God, and Jehovah alone,
Creator and ruler o'er all;
And we are His people, His sceptre we own;
His sheep, and we follow His call.

3 O enter His gates with thanksgiving and song,
Your vows in His temple proclaim;
His praise with melodious accordance prolong,
And bless His adorable name.

4 For good is the Lord, inexpressibly good,
And we are the work of His hand;
His mercy and truth from eternity stood,
And shall to eternity stand.

431   Eventide; or, the Chant.

1 Abide with me! Fast falls the eventide;
The darkness deepens; Lord, with me abide!
When other helpers fail, and comforts flee,
Help of the helpless, O abide with me!

2 Swift to its close ebbs out life's little day;
Earth's joys grow dim, its glories pass away;
Change and decay in all around I see;
O Thou who changest not abide with me!

3 I need Thy presence every passing hour;
What but Thy grace can foil the tempter's power!
Who like Thyself my guide and stay can be!
Through cloud and sunshine, O abide with me!

4 I fear no foe, with Thee at hand to bless;
Ills have no weight, and tears no bitterness:
Where is death's sting! where, grave, thy victory!
I triumph still, if thou abide with me!

5 Hold then Thy cross before my closing eyes;
Shine through the gloom, and point me to the skies;
Heaven's morning breaks, and earth's vain shadows flee:
In life, in death, O Lord, abide with me!

432   Eventide; or, the Chant.

1 Abide in me, O Lord, and I in Thee,
From this good hour, O leave me nevermore;
Then shall the discord cease, the wound be healed,
The life-long bleeding of the soul be o'er.

2 Abide in me; o'ershadow by Thy love
Each half-formed purpose and dark thought of sin;
Quench ere it rise each selfish, low desire,
And keep my soul as Thine, calm and divine.

3 As some rare perfume in a vase of clay,
Pervades it with a fragrance not its own,
So when Thou dwellest in a mortal soul,
All heaven's own sweetness seems around it thrown.

4 Abide in me: there have been moments blest
When I have heard Thy voice and felt Thy power;
Then evil lost its grasp; and passion hushed,
Owned the divine enchantment of the hour.

5 These were but seasons beautiful and rare;
Abide in me, and they shall ever be;
Fulfil at once Thy precept and my prayer,
Come, and abide in me, and I in Thee.

433   Sacrament.

1 Bread of the world in mercy broken,
Wine of the soul in mercy shed,
By whom the words of life were spoken,
And in whose death our sins are dead:

2 Look on the heart by sorrow broken,
Look on the tears by sinners shed,
And be Thy feast to us the token
That by Thy grace our souls are fed.

434   Chant.

1 My God, my Father, | while I | stray,
Far from my home, in | life's rough | way,
O teach me from my | heart to | say,
"Thy | will be | done."

2 Though dark my path, and | sad my | lot,
Let me be still and | murmur | not,
Or breathe the prayer di- | vinely | taught,
"Thy | will be | done."

3 What though in lonely | grief I | sigh
For friends beloved no | longer | nigh,
Submissive would I | still re- | ply,
"Thy | will be | done."

4 If Thou shouldst call me | to re- | sign
What most I prize, it | ne'er was | mine,
I only yield Thee | what is | Thine;
"Thy | will be | done."

5 Let but my fainting | heart be | blest
With Thy sweet Spirit | for its | guest,
My God, to Thee I | leave the | rest;
"Thy | will be | done."

6 Renew my will from | day to | day,
Blend it with Thine, and | take a- | way
All that now makes it | hard to | say,
"Thy | will be | done." Amen.

435

1 In us the hope of glory,
  O risen Lord, art Thou;
  The first-fruits of the Spirit
    Are in us now.

2 Yet still in dust and ashes
  Before Thy throne we kneel;
  And in our hearts is hidden
    Thy living seal.

3 The whole creation groaneth
  In prison-chains for Thee;
  O rend the veil asunder,
    And set us free!

4 Raise up Thy holy sleepers,
  And change Thy saints on earth,
  In all, as one, revealing
    The second birth!

5 O come in all Thy glory,
  Our great Immanuel!
  Come forth, our Prince and Saviour,
    With us to dwell!

6 Bring Thine eternal Sabbath,
  Bring Thine eternal day,
  And cause all grief and sighing
    To flee away!

7 To Thee, Almighty Father,
  O Saviour, unto Thee,
  To Thee, Creator-Spirit,
    All glory be!

436

1 One sweetly solemn thought
  Comes to me o'er and o'er:
  I'm nearer home to-day,
  Than I have been before;
  Nearer my Father's house,
  Where many mansions be,
  Nearer the great white throne,
  Nearer the crystal sea,

2 Nearer the bound of life,
  Where burdens are laid down,
  Nearer to leave the cross,
  And nearer to the crown;
  But lying dark between,
  And winding through the night,
  The deep and unknown stream
  Crossed ere we reach the light.

3 Jesus, confirm my trust;
  Strengthen the hand of faith
  To feel Thee, when I stand
  Upon the shore of death.
  Be near me when my feet
  Are slipping o'er the brink;
  For I am nearer home,
  Perhaps, than now I think.

437

1 My days are gliding swiftly by,
  And I, a pilgrim stranger,
  Would not detain them as they fly,
  Those hours of toil and danger;

  For O we stand on Jordan's strand,
  Our friends are passing over;
  And just before, the shining shore
  We may almost discover.

2 We'll gird our loins, my brethren dear,
  Our heavenly home discerning;
  Our absent Lord has left us word,
  Let every lamp be burning;

3 Should coming days be cold and dark,
  We need not cease our singing;
  That perfect rest naught can molest,
  Where golden harps are ringing;

4 Let sorrow's rudest tempest blow,
  Each cord on earth to sever;
  Our King says, Come, and there's our home,
  Forever, O forever!

438

1 Holy Ghost, the infinite!
 Shine upon our nature's night
 With Thy blessed inward light,
  Comforter Divine!

2 We are sinful, cleanse us, Lord;
 We are faint, Thy strength afford;
 Lost, until by Thee restored,
  Comforter Divine!

3 Like the dew Thy peace distil;
 Guide, subdue our wayward will,
 Things of Christ unfolding still,
  Comforter Divine!

4 In us, for us, intercede,
 And with voiceless groanings plead
 Our unutterable need,
  Comforter Divine!

5 In us "Abba, Father," cry,
 Earnest of our bliss on high,
 Seal of immortality,
  Comforter Divine!

6 Search for us the depths of God,
 Bear us up the starry road
 To the height of Thine abode,
  Comforter Divine!

439

1 Heirs of an immortal crown,
 Heed not every foeman's frown,
 Tread the powers of darkness down,
  Through Jehovah's might:
 Though they oft in wrath arise,
 Like the tempest of the skies,
 He can fill them with surprise,
  From his heavenly height.

2 Soldier, in the tented field
 Ply thy helmet, sword, and shield,
 Till the line of battle yield,
  And before thee flee;
 In thine armor, fearless stand,
 Girded by Jehovah's hand,
 Till within the promised land,
  He shall set thee free.

3 Jesus Christ, the Eternal Son
 Glorious Leader, bids us on;
 He the victory has won,
  We His praise prolong.
 Vanquished are the powers of hell,
 When He rose their kingdoms fell.
 Let the saints with rapture swell
  Heaven's exultant song.

440

1 Just as I am, without one plea
 But that Thy blood was | shed for | me,
 And that Thou bid'st me | come to | Thee,
  O Lamb of God, I come!

2 Just as I am, and waiting not
 To rid my soul of | one dark | blot,
 To Thee, whose blood can | cleanse each | spot,
  O Lamb of God, I come!

3 Just as I am, though tossed about
 With many a conflict, | many a | doubt,
 Fightings within, and | fears with- | out,
  O Lamb of God, I come!

4 Just as I am, poor, wretched, blind;
 Sight, riches, healing | of the | mind,
 Yea, all I need, in | Thee to | find,
  O Lamb of God, I come!

5 Just as I am, Thou wilt receive,
 Wilt welcome, pardon, | cleanse, re- | lieve;
 Because Thy promise | I be- | lieve,
  O Lamb of God, I come!

6 Just as I am, Thy love unknown
 Has broken every | barrier | down,
 Now, to be Thine, yea, | Thine a- | lone,
  O Lamb of God, I come!

441

1 O Paradise! O Paradise!
　Who doth not crave for rest!
　Who would not seek the happy land
　Where they that loved are blest:
　Where loyal hearts and true
　Stand ever in the light,
　All rapture through and through,
　In God's most holy sight.

2 O Paradise! O Paradise!
　I want to sin no more;
　I want to be as pure on earth
　As on thy spotless shore:
　Where loyal hearts and true, etc.

3 O Paradise! O Paradise!
　'Tis weary waiting here;
　I long to be where Jesus is,
　To feel, to see Him near:
　Where loyal hearts and true, etc.

4 O Paradise! O Paradise!
　I feel 'twill not be long;
　Patience! I almost think I hear
　Faint fragments of thy song!
　Where loyal hearts and true, etc.

442

1 Sing of Jesus, sing forever
　Of the love that changes never.
　Who, or what, from Him can sever
　　Those He makes His own!

2 With His blood the Lord hath bought them;
　When they knew Him not He sought them!
　And from all their wanderings brought them;
　　His the praise alone.

3 Through the desert Jesus leads them,
　With the bread of heaven He feeds them,
　And through all their way He speeds them
　　To their home above.

4 There they see the Lord who bought them,
　Him who came from heaven and sought them,
　Him who by His Spirit taught them,
　　Him they serve and love.

443

1 We are on our journey home,
　Where Christ our Lord is gone;
　We shall meet around His throne,
　When He makes His people one
　　In the New Jerusalem.

2 We can see that distant home,
　Though clouds rise dark between;
　Faith views the radiant dome,
　And a lustre flashes keen
　　From the New Jerusalem.

3 O glory shining far
　From the never-setting Sun!
　O trembling morning-star!
　Our journey's almost done
　　To the New Jerusalem.

4 O holy, heavenly home!
　O rest eternal there!
　When shall the exiles come
　Where they cease from earthly care
　　In the New Jerusalem?

5 Our hearts are breaking now
　Those mansions fair to see;
　O Lord, Thy heavens bow
　And raise us up with Thee,
　　To the New Jerusalem.

444

1 "Thy will be | done!"| In devious way
　The hurrying stream of | life may | run ;||
　Yet still our grateful hearts shall say, |
　　"Thy will be done."

2 "Thy will be | done!"| If o'er us shine
　A gladd'ning and a | prosp'rous | sun.||
　This prayer will make it more divine; |
　　"Thy will be | done."

3 "Thy will be done!"| Though shrouded o'er
　Our | path with | gloom,|| one comfort—one
　Is ours; to breathe, while we adore, |
　　"Thy will be done!"

[Close by repeating the first two measures—"Thy will be done."]

445

1 How firm a foundation, ye saints of the Lord,
Is laid for your faith in His excellent word!
What more can He say than to you He hath said,
Who unto the Saviour for refuge hath fled!

2 "Fear not, I am with thee, O be not dismayed,
For I am thy God, and will still give thee aid;
I'll strengthen thee, help thee, and cause thee to stand,
Upheld by my righteous, omnipotent hand.

3 "When through the deep waters I call thee to go,
The rivers of sorrow shall not overflow;
For I will be with thee thy troubles to bless,
And sanctify to thee thy deepest distress.

4 "When through fiery trials thy pathway shall lie,
My grace all-sufficient shall be thy supply;
The flame shall not hurt thee, I only design
Thy dross to consume, and thy gold to refine.

5 "E'en down to old age, all My people shall prove
My sovereign, eternal, unchangeable love;
And then, when gray hairs shall their temples adorn,
Like lambs they shall still in My bosom be borne.

6 "The soul that on Jesus hath leaned for repose
I will not, I will not desert to his foes;
That soul, though all hell should endeavor to shake,
I'll never, no never, no never forsake."

446

1 Stand fast in the faith! 'tis the mandate of God,
Once uttered in anguish, once written in blood;
From the cross of the Lord, from the throne in the sky,
It was breathed over earth, it is uttered on high.

2 Stand fast in the faith! there are those at thy side
Who can vanquish the foe in his ramparts of pride;
Be loyal, be valiant; thy heart to inspire,
Lo! the chariots of God, and the horses of fire.

3 Stand fast in the faith! though the conflict is hot,
The field hath no strife where thy Captain is not;
His eye is upon thee, thou hear'st what He saith:
"Ho! quit you like men, and stand fast in the faith."

4 Stand fast in the faith! though the faithless may flee,
We will peril our all, dear Redeemer, for Thee;
We will stand in the conflict, assured that Thine arm
Shall shield every soldier from peril and harm.

447

Psalm 104.

1 O worship the King, all glorious above,
O gratefully sing His power and His love;
Our shield and defender, the Ancient of days,
Pavilioned in splendor and girded with praise.

2 O tell of His might, O sing of His grace,
Whose robe is the light, whose canopy space;
His chariots of wrath the deep thunder-clouds form,
And dark is His path on the wings of the storm.

3 The earth, with its store of wonders untold,
Almighty, Thy power hath founded of old,
Hath stablished it fast by a changeless decree,
And round it hath cast like a mantle the sea.

4 Thy bountiful care what tongue can recite!
It breathes in the air, it shines in the light,
It streams from the hills, it descends to the plain,
And sweetly distils in the dew and the rain.

5 Frail children of dust, and feeble as frail,
In Thee do we trust, nor find Thee to fail;
Thy mercies how tender, how firm to the end,
Our Maker, Defender, Redeemer, and Friend!

6 O measureless Might, ineffable Love!
While angels delight to hymn Thee above,
The humbler creation, though feeble their lays,
With true adoration shall lisp to Thy praise.

448

1 Ye servants of God, your Master proclaim,
And publish abroad His wonderful name;
The name all-victorious of Jesus extol;
His kingdom is glorious, and rules over all.

2 God ruleth on high, almighty to save;
Yet still He is nigh, His presence we have;
The great congregation His triumph shall sing,
Ascribing salvation to Jesus our King.

3 "Salvation to God who sits on the throne,"
Let all cry aloud and honor the Son;
Immanuel's praises the angels proclaim,
Fall down on their faces, and worship the Lamb.

4 Then let us adore and give Him His right,
All glory and power, and wisdom and might;
All honor and blessing, with angels above,
And thanks never ceasing, and infinite love.

449

1 I would not live alway; I ask not to stay
Where storm after storm rises dark o'er the way;
The few lurid mornings that dawn on us here
Are enough for life's woes, full enough for its cheer.

2 I would not live alway; no, welcome the tomb;
Since Jesus hath lain there, I dread not its gloom;
There sweet be my rest, till He bid me arise
To hail Him in triumph descending the skies.

3 Who, who would live alway, away from his God!
Away from yon heaven, that blissful abode
Where the rivers of pleasure flow o'er the bright plains,
And the noontide of glory eternally reigns:

4 Where the saints of all ages in harmony meet,
Their Saviour and brethren transported to greet,
While the anthems of rapture unceasingly roll,
And the smile of the Lord is the feast of the soul.

450

Psalm 23.

1 The Lord is my Shepherd, no want shall I know;
I feed in green pastures, safe-folded I rest;
He leadeth my soul where the still waters flow,
Restores me when wandering, redeems when opprest.

2 Through the valley and shadow of death though I stray,
Since Thou art my Guardian, no evil I fear;
Thy rod shall defend me, Thy staff be my stay;
No harm can befall with my Comforter near.

3 In the midst of affliction my table is spread;
With blessings unmeasured my cup runneth o'er;
With perfume and oil Thou anointest my head;
O what shall I ask of Thy providence more!

4 Let goodness and mercy, my bountiful God,
Still follow my steps till I meet Thee above;
I seek, by the path which my forefathers trod
Through the land of their sojourn, Thy kingdom of love.

451

1 Come, ye disconsolate, where'er ye languish;
Come, at the shrine of God fervently kneel;
Here bring your wounded hearts, here tell your anguish;
Earth has no sorrow that Heaven cannot heal.

2 Joy of the desolate, Light of the straying,
Hope of the penitent, fadeless and pure;
Here speaks the Comforter, tenderly saying,
Earth has no sorrow that Heaven cannot cure.

3 Here see the Bread of Life; see waters flowing
Forth from the throne of God, pure from above;
Come to the feast of love, come, ever knowing
Earth has no sorrow but Heaven can remove.

452

1 Lead, kindly Light, amid the encircling gloom
  Lead Thou me on;
The night is dark and I am far from home,
  Lead Thou me on;
Keep Thou my feet; I do not ask to see
The distant scene; one step enough for me.

2 I was not ever thus, nor prayed that Thou
  Shouldst lead me on;
I loved to choose and see my path; but now
  Lead Thou me on:
I loved the garish day, and, spite of fears,
Pride ruled my will. Remember not past years!

3 So long Thy power has blessed me, sure it still
  Will lead me on
O'er moor and fen, o'er crag and torrent till
  The night is gone;
And with the morn those angel faces smile
Which I have loved long since, and lost awhile!

453

1 Great God, what do I see and hear!
The end of things created!
The Judge of man I see appear,
On clouds of glory seated;
The trumpet sounds, the graves restore
The dead which they contained before;
Prepare, my soul, to meet Him.

2 The dead in Christ shall first arise
At the last trumpet's sounding,
Caught up to meet Him in the skies,
With joy their Lord surrounding;
No gloomy fears their souls dismay;
His presence sheds eternal day
On those prepared to meet Him.

3 Great God, what do I see and hear!
The end of things created!
The Judge of man I see appear,
On clouds of glory seated.
Beneath His cross I view the day
When heaven and earth shall pass away,
And thus prepare to meet Him.

454

1 The voice of free grace cries, Escape to the mountain!
For Adam's lost race, Christ hath opened a fountain;
For sin and uncleanness and every transgression
His blood flows most freely in streams of salvation.
Hallelujah to the Lamb, who hath purchased our pardon,
We'll praise Him again when we pass over Jordan!

2 Ye souls that are wounded, to Jesus repair,
Now He calls you in mercy, and can you forbear!
Though your sins are increased as high as a mountain,
His blood can remove them, it flows from the fountain.

3 Now Jesus, our King, reigns triumphantly glorious;
O'er sin, death, and hell, He is more than victorious;
With shouting proclaim it, O trust in His passion,
He saves us most freely, O glorious salvation!

4 With joy shall we stand when escaped to the shore;
With harps in our hands we'll praise Him the more;
We'll range the sweet plains on the bank of the river
And sing of salvation forever and ever!

455

1 GLORY be to | God on | high, ∥ and on earth | peace, good- | will toward | men.
2 We praise Thee, we bless Thee, we | worship | Thee, ∥ we glorify Thee, we give thanks to | Thee for | Thy great | glory,
3 O Lord God, | heavenly | King, ∥ God the | Father | Al- | mighty.
4 O Lord, the only-begotten Son, | Jesus | Christ; ∥ O Lord God, Lamb of | God, Son | of the | Father,
5 That takest away the | sins · of the | world, ∥ have mercy | upon | us.
6 Thou that takest away the | sins · of the | world, ∥ have mercy | upon | us.
7 Thou that takest away the | sins · of the | world, ∥ re- | ceive our | prayer.
8 Thou that sittest at the right hand of | God the | Father, ∥ have mercy | upon | us.
9 For Thou | only · art | holy; ∥ Thou | only | art the | Lord;
10 Thou only, O Christ, with the | Holy | Ghost, ∥ art most high in the | glory of | God the | Father. ∥ A- | men. ∥

THE STRAIN UPRAISE.

456

1 The strain upraise of joy and praise, Alle- | lu- | ia; ∥ To the glory of their King shall the ransomed | people | sing, ∥ Alle- | lu- | ia, ∥ Alle- | lu- | ia. ∥
2 And the choirs that | dwell on | high, ∥ Shall re-echo | through the | sky, ∥ Alle- | lu- | ia, ∥ Alle- | lu- | ia. ∥
3 They in the rest of Para- | dise who | dwell, ∥ The blessed ones with joy the | chorus | swell, ∥ Alle- | lu- | ia, ∥ Alle- | lu- | ia. ∥
4 This is the strain, the eternal strain, the Lord Al- | mighty | loves, ∥ Alle- | lu- | ia, ∥ This is the song, the heavenly song, that Christ the ∥ King ap- | proves, ∥ Alle- | lu- | ia. ∥
5 Therefore we sing, both heart and voice a- | wak- | ing, ∥ Alle- | lu- | ia, ∥ And children's voices echo, answer | mak- | ing, ∥ Alle- | lu- | ia. ∥
6 Now from all men | be out- | poured, ∥ Alleluia | to the | Lord, ∥ With Alleluia | ever- | more, ∥ The Son and Spirit | we a- | dore. ∥
7 Praise be done to the | Three in ' One ∥ Alle- | lu- | ia, ∥ Alle- | lu- | ia, ∥ Alleluia— | A- | men. ∥

457
Psalm 148.

1 Praise | ye the | Lord.
Praise ye the Lord from the heavens : | praise Him | in the | heights.
2 Praise ye Him, | all His | angels :
Praise | ye Him, | all His | hosts.
3 Praise ye Him, | sun and | moon :
Praise Him | all ye | stars of | light.
4 Praise Him, ye | heaven of | heavens,
And ye waters that | be a- | bove the | heavens.
5 Let them praise the | name · of the | Lord :
For He commanded, | and they | were cre- | ated.
6 Kings of the earth, | and all | people ;
Princes, and all | judges | of the | earth ;
7 Both young men, and maidens ; | old · men, and | children :
Let them praise the | name— | of the | Lord :
8 For His name a- | lone is | excellent ;
His glory is a- | bove the | earth and | heaven.

458
Psalm 150.

1 Praise | ye the | Lord.
Praise God in His sanctuary ; praise Him in the | firma-ment | of His | power.
2 Praise Him for His | mighty | acts ;
Praise Him according | to His | excel-lent | greatness.
3 Praise Him with the | sound · of the | trumpet :
Praise Him | with the | psaltery · and | harp.
4 Praise Him with the | timbrel · and | dance :
Praise Him with stringed | instru- | ments and | organs.
5 Praise Him upon the | loud— | cymbals :
Praise Him upon the | high- — | sounding cymbals.
6 Let every thing that hath breath | praise the | Lord :
Praise | ye — | the — | Lord.
Glory be to the Father, and | to the | Son,
And | to the | Holy | Ghost ;
As it was in the beginning, is now, and | ever | shall be,
World | without | end. A- | men.

459
Psalm 100.

1 O be joyful in the Lord, | all ye | lands ;
Serve the Lord with gladness, and come before His | presence | with a | song.
2 Be ye sure that the Lord | He is | God ;
It is He that hath made us, and not we ourselves ; we are His people, | and the | sheep of · His | pasture.
3 O go your way into His gates with thanksgiving, and into His | courts with | praise ;
Be thankful unto Him, and | speak good | of His | name.
4 For the Lord is gracious, His mercy is | ever- | lasting,
And His truth endureth from gener- | ation to | gener- | ation.
Glory be to the Father, etc.

460
Psalm 95.

1 O come, let us sing un- | to the | Lord;
 Let us heartily rejoice in the | strength of | our sal- | vation.
2 Let us come before His presence | with thanks- | giving;
 And show ourselves | glad in | Him with | psalms.
3 For the Lord is a | great — | God;
 And a great | King a- | bove all | gods.
4 In His hands are all the corners | of the | earth;
 And the strength of the | hills is | His — | also.
5 The sea is His, | and He | made it;
 And His hands pre- | pared the | dry— | land.
6 O come, let us worship, | and fall | down;
 And kneel be- | fore the | Lord our | Maker:
7 For He is the | Lord our | God;
 And we are the people of His pasture and the | sheep of | His — | hand.
8 O worship the Lord in the | beauty of | holiness;
 Let the whole earth | stand in | awe of | Him:
9 For He cometh, for He cometh, to | judge the | earth;
 And with righteousness to judge the world, and the | people | with His | truth.
10 Glory be to the Father, and | to the | Son,
 And | to the | Holy | Ghost;
 As it was in the beginning, is now, and | ever | shall be,
 World | without | end. A- | men.

461
Psalm 98.

1 O sing unto the | Lord · a new | song,
 For He | hath done | marvellous | things.
2 With His own right hand, and with His | holy | arm,
 Hath He | gotten Him- | self the | victory.
3 The Lord declared | His sal- | vation,
 His righteousness hath He openly showed | in the | sight · of the | heathen.
4 He hath remembered His mercy and truth toward the | house of | Israel,
 And all the ends of the world have seen the sal- | vation | of our | God.
5 Show yourselves joyful unto the Lord, | all ye | lands,
 Sing, re- | joice and | give — | thanks.
6 Praise the Lord up- | on the | harp,
 Sing to the harp with a | psalm of | thanks- | giving;
7 With trumpets | also, and | shawms,
 O show yourselves joyful be- | fore the | Lord the | King.
8 Let the sea make a noise, and all that | therein | is,
 The round world, and | they that | dwell there- | in.
9 Let the floods clap their hands, and let the hills be joyful together be- | fore the | Lord,
 For He | cometh to | judge the | earth.
10 With righteousness shall He | judge the | world,
 And the | people | with | equity.
 Glory be to the Father, etc.

462

Psalm 103.

1 Bless the Lord, | O my | soul :
  And all that is within me, | bless His | holy | Name.
2 Bless the Lord, | O my | soul,
  And for- | get not | all His | benefits :
3 Who forgiveth all | thine in- | iquities,
  Who | healeth all | thy dis- | eases ;
4 Who redeemeth thy life | from de- | struction ;
  Who crowneth thee with loving- | kindness and | tender | mercies ;
5 The Lord is merci- | ful and | gracious,
  Slow to anger, and | plente- | ous in | mercy.
6 He hath not dealt with us | after our | sins ;
  Nor rewarded us ac- | cording to | our in- | iquities.
7 For as the heaven is high a- | bove the | earth,
  So great is His mercy toward | them that | fear — | Him.
8 As far as the east is | from the | west,
  So far hath He removed | our trans- | gressions | from us.
9 Like as a father | pitieth · his | children,
  So the Lord pitieth | them that | fear — | Him.
10 Bless the Lord, all His works, in all places of | His do- | minion :
   Bless the Lord, | O— | my— | soul.

463

1 Blessed be the Lord | God of | Israel,
  For He hath visited | and re- | deemed His | people ;
2 And hath raised up a horn of sal- | vation | for us,
  In the house | of His | servant | David :
3 As He spake by the mouth of His | holy | prophets,
  Which have been | since the | world be- | gan ;
4 That we should be saved | from our | enemies,
  And from the | hand of | all that | hate us.
5 Glory be to the Father, and | to the | Son,
  And | to the | Holy | Ghost ;
  As it was in the beginning, is now, and | ever | shall be,
  World | without | end. A- | men.

464

1 The Lord is my strength and song,
  And is become | my sal- | vation.
2 The voice of rejoicing and salvation
  Is in the tabernacles of the righteous :
  The right | hand · of the | Lord · doeth | valiantly.
3 Open to me the gates of righteousness :
  I will go into them, and I will | praise the | Lord ;
4 This gate of the Lord,
  Into | which the | righteous—shall | enter.
5 I will praise Thee ; for Thou hast heard me
  And art become | my sal- | vation.
6 O give thanks unto the Lord, for He is good ;
  For His | mer-cy en- | dureth— for- | ever.

  Glory be to the Father, and to the Son,
    And to the Holy Ghost ;
  As it was in the beginning, is now, and ever shall be,
    World without end. Amen.

465
Psalm 67.

1 God be merciful unto | us, and | bless us;
And cause His | face to | shine up- | on us;

2 That Thy way may be | known upon | earth,
Thy saving | health a- | mong all | nations.

3 Let the people | praise Thee, ·O | God;
Let | all the | people | praise Thee.

4 O let the nations be glad and | sing for | joy:
For Thou shalt judge the people righteously, and govern the | nations | upon | earth.

5 Let the people | praise Thee, ·O | God;
Let | all the | people | praise Thee.

6 Then shall the earth | yield her | increase;
And God, even | our own | God, shall | bless us.

7 God | shall — | bless us;
And all the ends of the | earth shall | fear — | Him.

Glory be to the Father, etc.

466
Psalm 121.

1 I will lift up mine eyes unto the hills, from whence | cometh ·my | help.
My help cometh from the Lord, | which made | heaven ·and | earth.

2 He will not suffer thy foot to be moved: He that keepeth thee | will not | slumber.
Behold, He that keepeth Israel shall | neither | slumber ·nor | sleep.

3 The Lord is thy keeper: the Lord is thy shade upon | thy right | hand.
The sun shall not smite thee by day, | nor the | moon by | night.

4 The Lord shall preserve thee from all evil; He shall pre- | serve thy | soul.
The Lord shall preserve thy going out and thy coming in from this time forth, and | even ·for | ever- | more.

Glory be to the Father, etc.

467
Psalm 23.

1 The Lord is my Shepherd, I | shall not | want.
He maketh me to lie down in green pastures;
He leadeth me be- | side the | still— | waters.

2 He re- | storeth ·my | soul:
He leadeth me in the paths of righteousness | for His | name's | sake.

3 Yea, though I walk through the valley of the shadow of death, I will | fear no | evil:
For Thou art with me, Thy rod and Thy | staff they | comfort | me.

4 Thou preparest a table before me in the presence | of mine | enemies;
Thou anointest my head with oil; | my cup | runneth | over.

5 Surely goodness and mercy shall follow me all the | days of ·my | life:
And I will dwell in the | house ·of the | Lord for | ever.

468
Psalm 90.

1 LORD, Thou hast been our | dwelling- | place,
   In | all— | gener- | ations.

2 Before the mountains were brought forth, or ever Thou hadst formed the | earth · and the | world,
   Even from everlasting to ever- | lasting, | Thou art | God.

3 Thou turnest man | to de- | struction;
   And sayest, Re- | turn, ye | children · of | men.

4 For a thousand years in Thy sight are but as yesterday, | when · it is | past,
   And as a | watch— | in the | night.

5 Thou carriest them away as with a flood; they are | as a | sleep:
   In the morning they are like | grass which | groweth | up.

6 In the morning it flourisheth, and | groweth | up;
   In the evening it is cut | down, and | wither- | eth.

7 Who knoweth the power | of Thine | anger!
   Even according to Thy fear, | so— | is Thy | wrath.

8 So teach us to | number · our | days,
   That we may apply our | hearts— | unto | wisdom. Amen.

469
Psalm 46.

1 GOD is our | refuge · and | strength,
   A very | present | help in | trouble.

2 Therefore will not we fear, though the | earth be | removed,
   And though the mountains be carried | into · the | midst · of the | sea.

3 Though the waters thereof | roar · and be | troubled,
   Though the mountains | shake · with the | swelling · there- | of.

4 There is a river, the streams whereof shall make glad the | city of | God,
   The holy place of the tabernacles | of the | Most— | High.

5 God is in the midst of her; she | shall not · be | moved:
   God shall help her, | and— | that right | early.

6 The heathen raged, the | kingdoms · were | moved:
   He uttered His | voice, the | earth— | melted.

7 The Lord of | hosts is | with us ;
   The God of | Jacob | is our | refuge.
   Glory be to the Father, etc.

470

1 THEN will I sprinkle clean | water · up- | on you,
   And | ye shall | be— | clean:

2 A new heart also | will I | give you,
   And a new spirit | will I | put with- | in you:

3 And I will take away the stony heart | out of · your | flesh,
   And I will | give you · a | heart of | flesh:

4 And I will put my | Spirit · with- | in you,
   And ye shall | keep my | judgments, · and | do them.

5 I will pour my Spirit up- | on thy | seed,
   And my | blessing · up- | on thine | offspring:

6 And they shall spring up as a- | mong the | grass,
   As willows | by the | water- | courses.

7 For the promise is unto you, and | to your | children,
   And to all that are afar off, even as many as the | Lord our | God shall | call.
   Glory be to the Father, and | to the | Son,
   And | to the | Holy | Ghost;
   As it was in the beginning, is now, and | ever | shall be,
   World | without | end. A | men.

TE DEUM LAUDAMUS.

471

1 We praise | Thee, O | God : || we acknowledge | Thee to | be the | Lord ; 2
3 To Thee all Angels | cry a- | loud, || the Heavens, and | all the | Powers there- | in. 4
6 The glorious company of the Apostles | praise — | Thee ; || the goodly fellowship of the | Prophets | praise — | Thee ; 7
8 The Father of an | infi-nite | Majesty ; || Thine adorable, | true, and | only | Son ; 9

2 All the earth doth | worship | Thee, || the | Father | ever- | lasting. 3
4 To Thee Cherubim and | Sera- | phim, || con- | tinual- | ly do | cry, 5
7 The noble army of Martyrs | praise — | Thee ; || the Holy Church throughout all the world | doth ac- | knowledge | Thee, 8
9 Also the | Holy | Ghost, || the | Com- — | fort- — | er. `10.

5 Ho-ly, Ho-ly, Ho-ly, Lord God of Sab-a-oth,

Heaven and earth are full of the maj-es-ty of Thy glo-ry 6

TE DEUM LAUDAMUS. Concluded.

10 Thou art the King of | glory, · O | Christ; || Thou art the ever- | lasting | Son · of the | Father.
11 When Thou tookest upon Thee to de- | liver | man, || Thou didst humble Thyself to be | born — | of a | virgin.
12 When thou hadst overcome the | sharpness · of | death, || Thou didst open the kingdom of | heaven · to | all be- | lievers.
13 Thou sittest at the right | hand of | God, || in the | glory | of the | Father.
14 We believe that | Thou shalt | come, || shalt | come to | be our | Judge.
15 We therefore pray Thee | help Thy | servants, || whom Thou hast redeemed | with Thy | precious | blood.
16 Make them to be numbered | with Thy | saints, || in | glory | ever- | lasting.
17 O Lord, save Thy people, and | bless Thine | heritage; || govern them, and | lift them | up for- | ever.
18 Day by day we | magni-fy | Thee, || and we worship Thy Name ever, | world with- | out — | end.
19 Vouch- | safe, O | Lord, || to keep us | this day | without | sin.
20 O Lord, have | mercy · up- | on us, || have | mercy | upon | us.
21 O Lord, let Thy mercy | be up- | on us, || as our | trust — | is in | Thee.

22 O Lord, in Thee, in Thee have I trust-ed; let me nev-er

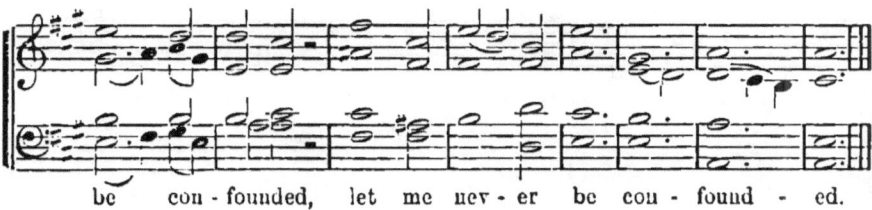

be con-founded, let me nev-er be con-found-ed.

116   CHRISTIAN PRAISE.

BELINA. 7s. Double.

3.
O God, our light! to Thee we bow;
Within all shadows standest Thou;
Give deeper calm than night can bring;
Give sweeter songs than lips can sing.

4.
Life's tumults we must meet again,
We cannot at the shrine remain;
But in the spirits' secret cell
May hymn and prayer for ever dwell.

THE LORD IS MY STRENGTH.

120   CHRISTIAN PRAISE.

THE LORD IS MY STRENGTH. Continued.

ness, that I may go in to them, and give thanks, give
that I may go..................
ness,.... that I... may go

thanks, give thanks un - to the Lord.
thanks un - to............ the Lord, The same stone which the
thanks, give thanks.... un - to the Lord.
thanks, give thanks un - to the Lord.

Grave. ♩ = 60.

build-ers re - fus - ed, The same stone which the builders re - fus - ed,...

♩ = 60.

.... is be - come the head stone in the cor - ner, is be - come the

3. Here beneath a virtuous sway,
May we cheerfully obey,
Never feel oppression's rod,
Ever own and worship God.

4. Hark the voice of nature sings,
Praises to the King of kings,
Let us join the choral song,
And the grateful notes prolong.

BLESSED IS HE.

BLESSED IS HE. Continued.

THE LORD IS MY SHEPHERD.

Sing the Alto as Solo (except last five measures) then Da Capo, the other parts delicately accompanying the Alto.

The Lord is my shep-herd, I shall not want, He mak-eth me to lie down, lie down in green pas-tures, He lead-eth me,.... lead-eth me...... be-side the still.. wa-ters: He re-stor-eth my soul, He re-stor-eth my soul, He lead-eth me, He lead-eth me in the paths of right-eous-ness

DOXOLOGIES.

1 L. M.
Praise God, from whom all blessings flow!
Praise Him all creatures here below!
Praise Him above, ye heavenly host!
Praise Father, Son, and Holy Ghost!

2 L. M.
To God the Father, God the Son,
And God the Spirit, three in one,
Be honor, praise, and glory given,
By all on earth and all in heaven.

3 C. M.
To Father, Son, and Holy Ghost,
The God whom we adore;
Be glory, as it was, is now,
And shall be evermore.

4 C. M.
Let God the Father, and the Son,
And Spirit, be adored,
Where there are works to make Him known,
Or saints to love the Lord.

5 S. M.
To the eternal Three,
In will and essence One;
To Father, Son, and Spirit be
Coequal honors done.

6 S. M.
To God, the Father, Son,
And Spirit, glory be,
As was and is, and shall remain
Through all eternity.

7 7s.
Sing we to our God above
Praise eternal as His love;
Praise Him, all ye heavenly host,
Father, Son, and Holy Ghost.

8 8s & 7s.
Praise the God of our salvation,
Praise the Father's boundless love,
Praise the Lamb, our expiation,
Praise the Spirit from above.

9 8s & 7s, Double.
Praise the God of our salvation:
Praise the Father's boundless love;
Praise the Lamb, our expiation;
Praise the Spirit from above;
Author of the new creation,
Him by whom our spirits live;
Undivided adoration
To the One Jehovah give.

10 8s, 7s & 4s.
Glory be to God the Father!
Glory be to God the Son!
Glory be to God the Spirit!
Great Jehovah, Three in One:
Glory, glory,
While eternal ages run.

11 H. M.
To God the Father's throne
Perpetual honors raise;
Glory to God the Son,
And to the Spirit praise:
With all our powers, eternal King,
Thy name we sing, while faith adores.

12 6s & 4s.
To the great One in Three,
The highest praises be,
Hence, evermore;
His sovereign majesty
May we in glory see,
And to eternity
Love and adore.

TOPICAL INDEX.

I. GOD, TRIUNE, 2, 336, 337, 341, 362, 380, 395, 414, 428, 455, 456, 471.
  THE FATHER, 7, 12, 65, 121, 200, 220, 252, 296, 390, 392, 413, 434, 444.
  ALMIGHTY, 12, 253.
    OMNISCIENT, 68.
    ETERNAL, 69, 149.
  MAKER OF HEAVEN AND EARTH, 1, 3, 4, 28, 116, 227.
    PROVIDENCE OF, 1, 3, 4, 7, 12, 20, 235, 255, 270, 302, 358, 389, 392, 445, 447.
    GRACE OF, 71, 135, 168, 186, 235, 238, 248, 252, 255, 264, 270, 289, 316, 348, 445, 454.
    PRAISE TO, 1, 3, 4, 5, 6, 7, 8, 9, 14, 15, 16, 17, 18, 19, 21, 27, 31, 32, 33, 44, 94, 96, 97, 108, 112, 113, 114, 115, 116, 118, 137, 144, 150, 152, 164, 192, 227, 252, 273, 274, 289, 294, 302, 328, 331, 334, 336, 362, 380, 386, 390, 417, 429, 447;
      (*The following in prose,*) 455, 456, 457, 458, 459, 460, 461, 462, 463, 464, 465, 466, 467, 468, 470, 471.

II. JESUS, 2, 16, 50, 104, 136, 151, 156, 167, 169, 170, 171, 332, 411, 442.
  CHRIST, HIS ONLY-BEGOTTEN SON,
    ALL, 140, 286, 406, 411.
    BLOOD OF, 181, 183, 187, 454.
    CROSS OF, 208, 338, 347.
    DAYSPRING, 129, 170, 240, 297, 310.
    EXAMPLE, 74, 104.
    FRIEND, 354.
    GRATITUDE TO, 206, 217, 218, 235, 238, 250, 331, 332.
    HELPER, 86, 102, 357, 373, 406.
    IN US, 47, 144, 194, 241, 244, 432.
    INTERCEDING, 58, 339.
    KING, 11, 22, 117, 119, 142, 230, 356, 361, 377, 383, 403, 424, 448, 454.
    KNOCKING, 87.
    LAMB OF GOD, 250, 345, 416, 440, 454.
    LIFE, 37, 57, 66, 121, 194, 198, 201, 220, 244, 312, 314, 342, 407, 435.
    LIGHT, 103, 201, 312, 452.
    LITANY TO, 323, 326, 409.
    LOVE OF, 56, 86, 100, 111, 218, 243, 264, 316, 342, 442.
    LOVE TO, 76, 104, 243, 332.

TOPICAL INDEX.

    Merits of, 51, 214, 345.
    Prayer to, 406, 418.
    Presence of, 47, 143, 166, 167, 169, 170, 357, 358, 374, 413, 435, 445, 448.
    Priest, 41, 37, 174, 383, 387.
    Prophet, 383.
    Redeemer, 55, 58.
    Refuge, 203, 255, 303.
    Rest, 201.
    Righteousness, 45, 51, 214.
    Rock, 256, 299, 316.
    Saviour, 41, 172, 173, 187, 217, 381, 418.
    Shepherd, 98, 182, 184, 258, 267, 307, 315, 450.
    Substitute, 183, 187, 214, 250.
    Sympathizer, 174.
    Truth, 198.
    Union with, 241, 296, 407.
    Way, 110, 198.
  Our Lord, 30, 40, 66, 154, 406, 412.
III. WHO WAS CONCEIVED BY THE HOLY GHOST, BORN OF THE VIRGIN MARY, 38, 122, 123, 126, 128, 165, 206, 226, 278, 335, 363, 379, 455.
    Epiphany, 35, 300, 425.
    Transfiguration, 54.
    Triumphal Entry, 23.
IV. SUFFERED UNDER PONTIUS PILATE, 88, 89, 324, 404.
  WAS CRUCIFIED, DEAD, AND BURIED; HE DESCENDED INTO HELL, 73, 90, 187, 295, 298, 299, 313, 347, 372, 400.
V. THE THIRD DAY HE ROSE AGAIN FROM THE DEAD, 55, 59, 120, 141, 275, 277, 279, 287, 387.
VI. HE ASCENDED INTO HEAVEN, 37, 95, 118, 131, 275, 284, 285, 361, 388, 415.
  AND SITTETH AT THE RIGHT HAND OF GOD THE FATHER, 11, 16, 21, 22, 24, 30, 34, 55, 117, 119, 339.
VII. FROM THENCE HE SHALL COME, 11, 17, 121, 123, 124, 129, 268, 282, 283, 304, 356, 359, 369, 370, 371, 377, 396, 402, 408, 424, 435, 453.
  TO JUDGE THE QUICK AND THE DEAD, 11, 91, 92, 213, 215, 371, 453.
VIII. THE HOLY GHOST.
    Invoked, 24, 63, 99, 101, 177, 178, 254, 257, 317, 419.
    The Life-Giver, 72, 101, 220, 320, 435.
    Comforter, 72, 438, 451.
    Guide, 63, 72, 438, 452.
    Sanctifier, 254, 342, 360, 438.
    Who spake by the Prophets, 26, 52, 70, 155, 193, 195, 219, 237.
IX. THE HOLY CATHOLIC CHURCH, 37, 70, 107, 133, 139, 146, 229, 230, 234, 239, 249, 330, 365, 430.
    The House of God, 17, 31, 46, 65, 80, 107, 132, 134, 139, 146, 147, 148, 228, 234, 252, 269, 270, 271, 391, 429.
  THE COMMUNION OF SAINTS, 79, 97, 121, 126, 138, 212, 229, 242, 245, 261, 265.
    In Worship:
      Opening, 80, 148.
      Closing, 83, 103, 225, 376.

TOPICAL INDEX.

The Lord's Supper, 41, 57, 88, 188, 189, 199, 202, 261, 262, 319, 325, 341, 343, 405, 433, 451.

Holy Baptism, 77, 82, 184, 185, 263, 351, 470.

Prayer, 64, 80, 83, 109, 111, 125, 143, 179, 180, 196, 197, 200, 203, 208, 209, 211, 234, 251, 256, 318, 322, 352, 406, 412, 418, 420.

Praise, 97, 125, 130, 142, 217, 221, 222, 229, 272, 273, 274, 336, 337, 378, 381, 414, 416, 442, 448, 454, 456.

    Morning, 29, 44, 67, 68, 106, 147, 210, 240, 297, 310, 311.

    Evening, 44, 49, 53, 59, 67, 68, 75, 106, 175, 243, 260, 309, 321, 349, 431.

    The Lord's Day, 43, 48, 120, 134, 232, 236, 271, 293, 301, 305, 306, 311, 382, 384, 395.

    Anniversary Days, 25, 61, 62, 137, 276, 292, 294, 327, 329, 422

    National Days, 105, 137, 276, 328, 421, 423.

IN WORK:

    The Christian Pilgrimage, 145, 158, 204, 251, 280, 288, 323, 333, 338, 352, 357, 375, 400, 436, 443.

    The Christian Conflict, 13, 40, 64, 102, 127, 157, 158, 208, 223, 224, 245, 248, 259, 338, 373, 393, 439, 445, 446.

    The Christian Ministry, 231.

    Christian Missions, 22, 38, 117, 119, 129, 216, 225, 281, 304, 364, 366, 394, 396, 401, 403.

    Invitation, 308, 385, 451.

    Contrition, 84, 85, 86, 344, 440.

    Confession, 36, 39, 42, 50, 60, 190, 411.

    Consecration, 148, 241, 243, 244, 245, 355, 367, 440.

X. THE FORGIVENESS OF SINS, 40, 45, 51, 52, 58, 59, 60, 64, 65, 111, 130, 154, 181, 201, 203, 214, 248, 250, 286, 296, 299, 309, 312, 316, 332, 333, 338, 344, 345, 346, 372, 373, 409, 411, 418, 440, 445, 454, 455.

XI. THE RESURRECTION OF THE BODY,

    (DEATH AND,) 36, 69, 78, 81, 93, 204, 205, 207, 247, 266, 410, 449.

XII. THE LIFE EVERLASTING, 66, 296, 353.

HEAVEN, 24, 159, 162, 176, 289.

    Inhabitants of, 138, 291, 340.

    Anticipated, 36, 43, 44, 121, 143, 164, 166, 191, 246, 259, 264, 398, 400, 408, 420, 426, 427, 436, 437, 441, 443, 449.

THE NEW JERUSALEM, 124, 160, 161, 397, 399.

ALPHABETICAL INDEX OF FIRST LINES.

First Line	Author	Page
Abide in me, O Lord	Harriet B. Stowe	101
Abide with me, fast falls the eventide	Lyte	101
A broken heart, my God, my King	Watts	21
A charge to keep I have	Wesley	57
Again as evening shadow falls	S. Longfellow	118
A glory gilds the sacred page	Cowper	36
Alas! and did my Saviour bleed	Watts	43
All hail the power of Jesus' name	Perronet	23
All people that on earth do dwell	Kethe	4
Amazing grace, how sweet the sound	Newton	43
Am I a soldier of the cross!	Watts	36
And did the holy and the just	Steele	42
Angels from the realms of glory	Montgomery	82
Angels, roll the rock away	Scott	62
Another six days' work is done	Stennett	13
A parting hymn we sing	Sarah F. Adams	59
Arise, O King of grace, arise	Watts	32
Arise, ye people, and adore		28
Ask ye what great thing	Monsell	65
Asleep in Jesus, blessed sleep	Mary Mackay	20
As pants the hart for cooling streams	Lyte	39
As with gladness men of old	W. C. Dix	68
Awake, and sing the song	Hammond	
Awake, my soul, and with the sun	Ken	9
Awake, my soul, in joyful lays	Medley	26
Awake, my soul, stretch every nerve	Doddridge	30
Awake, my tongue, thy tribute bring	Needham	5
Awake, ye saints, awake	Doddridge	87
Before Jehovah's awful throne	Watts	4
Behold a stranger 's at the door	Grigg	21
Behold the morning sun	Watts	54
Be joyful in God, all ye lands	Montgomery	100
Be thou exalted, O my God	Watts	4
Blessed are the sons of God	Joseph Humphreys	67
Blessed be the Lord God of Israel	(Chant.)	112
Blessed is he who cometh. (Adaptation.)		123, 124, 125
Blessed Saviour, Thee I love	G. Duffield, Jr.	67
Bless, O my soul, the living God	Watts	10
Bless the Lord, O my soul	(Chant.)	112
Blest are the sons of peace	Watts	57
Blest be the tie that binds	Fawcett	55
Blest be Thy love, dear Lord	Austin	55
Blest Comforter Divine	"H."	58
Blow ye the trumpet	Wesley	88
Bread of heaven, on Thee we feed	Conder	72
Bread of the world in mercy broken	Heber	101
Brightest and best of the sons	Heber	99
Call Jehovah thy salvation	Montgomery	81
Cast thy burden on the Lord		71
Children of the heavenly King	Cennick	65
Christ, of all my hopes the ground	Wyndham	71
Christ, the Lord, is risen to-day, Our	Wesley	63
Christ, the Lord, is risen to-day, Sons	Wesley	63
Christ, whose glory fills the sky	Wesley	67
Come, dearest Lord, descend	Watts	13
Come, every pious heart	Stennett	87
Come, gracious Spirit	Simon Browne	17
Come, Holy Ghost, all-quickening fire	Wesley	21
Come, Holy Spirit, come	Hart	58
Come, Holy Spirit, heavenly dove	Watts	41
Come, let us join our cheerful songs	Watts	29
Come, let us join our friends above	Wesley	30
Come, Lord, and tarry not	Bonar	60
Come, my soul, thy suit	Newton	72
Come, O my soul, in sacred lays	Blacklock	7
Come, sound His praise abroad	Watts	52
Come, thou almighty King		96
Come, thou fount of every blessing	Robinson	79
Come, thou long-expected Jesus	Wesley	81
Come to Calvary's holy mountain	Montgomery	70
Come, we that love the Lord	Watts	52
Come, ye disconsolate	Moore	107
Come, ye thankful people, come	Alford	66
Come, ye that love the Saviour's name	Steele	33
Commit thou all thy griefs	Gerhard, J. Wesley	56
Creator Spirit, by whose Veni, Creator, Dryden		24
Crowns of glory ever bright	Kelly	64
Dear refuge of my weary soul	Steele	46
Dear Saviour, if these lambs should stray	Hyde	20
Dear Saviour, we are thine	Doddridge	53
Deep in our hearts let us	Watts	21
Descend from heaven, immortal Dove	Watts	8
Dismiss us with Thy blessing, Lord	Hart	20
Early, my God, without delay	Watts	48
Eternal source of every joy	Doddridge	16
Eternal Spirit, we confess	Watts	18
Far as Thy name	Watts	54
Father, in these reveal Thy Son	Wesley	19
Father, whate'er of earthly bliss	Steele	45
Father, while we break this bread	Pierpont	73
For all Thy saints, O Lord	Mant	60
Forbid them not, the Saviour	Hastings	42
Forever with the Lord	Montgomery	56
From all that dwell below the skies	Watts	7
From every earthly pleasure	Ethel Davis	91
From every stormy wind that blows	Stowell	26
From Greenland's icy mountains	Heber	92
From the cross, uplifted	Haweis	67
Gently, Lord, O gently	Hastings	80
Give me the wings of faith	Watts	32
Give thanks to God, He reigns above	Watts	7
Give to our God immortal praise	Watts	6
Glorious things of thee are spoken	Newton	75
Glory be to God on high	(Chant.)	109
Glory be to God the Father	Bonar	82
Glory to God on high	Allen	96
Glory to Thee, my God, this night	Ken	14
God be merciful unto us	(Chant.)	113
God bless our native land	J. S. Dwight	98
God in His earthly temple lays	Watts	26
God in the Gospel of His Son	Beddome	14
God is gone up on high	Wesley	88
God is our refuge and strength	(Chant.)	114
God is the refuge of His saints	Watts	18
God most mighty, sovereign Lord	Harbaugh	74
God moves in a mysterious way	Cowper	27
God, my supporter and my hope	Watts	35
God of mercy, God of grace	Lyte	68
God of the sunlight hours		40
Grace, 'tis a charming sound	Doddridge	53
Gracious Spirit, Dove divine	Stocker	72

INDEX OF FIRST LINES.

First Line	Author	Page
Great God, attend while Zion sings	Watts.	10
Great God, how infinite art Thou	Watts.	27
Great God, indulge my humble claim	Watts.	17
Great God, let all our tuneful	Heginbotham.	8
Great God, to Thee my evening song	Steele.	16
Great God, we sing that mighty	Doddridge.	16
Great God, what do I see	Ringwald, Collyer.	108
Great God, whose universal sway	Watts.	10
Great is the Lord our God	Watts.	52
Great One in Three, Great Three in One		4
Guide me, O thou	William Williams.	85
Hail, my ever-blessed Jesus	Wingrove.	75
Hail, the day that sees Him rise	Wesley.	64
Hail, thou once despised Jesus	Bakewell.	78
Hail to the Lord's Anointed	Montgomery.	92
Hark! hark the notes of joy		86
Hark! ten thousand harps and voices	Kelly.	81
Hark! that shout of rapturous joy	Kelly.	64
Hark! the glad sound, the Saviour	Doddridge.	31
Hark! the herald angels sing	Wesley.	63
Hark! the song of jubilee	Montgomery.	64
Hark! the sound of holy voices	Wordsworth.	76
Hark! the voice of love and mercy	Evans (?).	84
Hark! what mean those holy voices	Cowper.	76
Hasten, Lord, the glorious time	Lyte.	63
He lives, the great Redeemer lives	Steele.	15
Heirs of an immortal	Hastings, Wardwell.	103
Heralds of creation, cry	Montgomery.	65
He reigns, the Lord, the Saviour reigns	Watts.	6
High in yonder realms of light	Raffles.	65
Holy, holy, holy, Lord God Almighty	Heber.	100
Holy Ghost, the Infinite		103
Holy Ghost, with light divine	Reed.	72
How beauteous are their feet	Watts.	58
How blest the righteous, when	Barbauld.	20
How blest the sacred tie	Barbauld.	20
How calm and beautiful the morn	Hastings.	61
How charming is the place	Stennett.	53
How did my heart rejoice to hear	Watts.	34
How firm a foundation, ye saints	Keith (?).	105
How gentle God's commands	Doddridge.	58
How happy every child of grace	Wesley.	33
How pleased and blest was I	Watts.	61
How pleasant, how divinely fair	Watts.	52
How precious is the book divine	Fawcett.	44
How sweet and awful is the place	Watts.	46
How sweet, how heavenly is the sight	Swain.	48
How sweet the name of Jesus sounds	Newton.	40
How sweet to leave the world awhile	Kelly.	20
If human kindness meets return	Noel.	89
I heard the voice of Jesus	Bonar.	46
I know no life divided		93
I know that my Redeemer lives	Medley.	15
I lay my sins on Jesus	Bonar.	95
I'll praise my Maker with my breath	Watts.	23
I love, I love Thee, Lord most high	Xavier.	19
I love Thy kingdom, Lord	T. Dwight.	57
I love to steal a while away	P. H. Brown.	41
I'm not ashamed to own my Lord	Watts.	36
In all my Lord's appointed ways	Ryland.	36
In the cross of Christ I glory	Bowring.	77
In the name of God the Father	Hewett.	77
In this calm, impressive hour	Hastings.	70
In this world of sin and sorrow		80
In us the hope of glory	Eddis.	102
It came upon the midnight clear	Sears.	38
It is not death to die	Malan, Bethune.	56
I've found the pearl of greatest price	Mason.	39
I will lift up mine eyes	(Chant.)	113
I would not live alway	Muhlenberg.	107
Jehovah reigns, He dwells in light	Watts.	5
Jehovah reigns, His throne is high	Watts.	5
Jerusalem, my happy	Urbs beata, "F. P. B."	37
Jerusalem the golden	Bernard, Neale.	91
Jerusalem the glorious	Bernard, Neale.	91
Jesus, and shall it ever be	Grigg.	14
Jesus, at whose supreme command	Wesley.	45
Jesus comes to souls rejoicing	Thring.	83
Jesus, enthroned and glorified	Z. Eddy.	50
Jesus, full of all compassion	Turner.	78
Jesus, hail! enthroned in glory	Bakewell.	77
Jesus, I live to Thee	Harbaugh.	55
Jesus, immortal King, arise	Seymour.	28
Jesus, I my cross have taken	Lyte.	80
Jesus invites His saints	Watts.	59
Jesus, lover of my soul	Wesley.	69
Jesus, lover of my soul	(Adaptation.)	116
Jesus, my all, to heaven is gone	Cennick.	26
Jesus, my Lord, my God, my all	Faber.	25
Jesus my Shepherd is	Bonar.	60
Jesus shall reign where'er the sun	Watts.	8
Jesus spreads His banner o'er us	R. Hart.	78
Jesus, these eyes have never seen	Ray Palmer.	39
Jesus, the very thought	Bernard, Caswall.	39
Jesus, Thou art the sinner's friend	Burnham.	43
Jesus, Thou joy of loving	Bernard, Palmer.	15
Jesus, Thy blood and	Zinzendorf, J. Wesley.	13
Jesus, Thy boundless love	Gerhard, J. Wesley.	24
Jesus, Thy boundless love to me	(L. M.)	15
Join all the glorious names	Watts.	87
Joy to the world, the Lord is come	Watts.	8
Just as I am, without one plea	Charlotte Elliott.	103
Keep silence, all created things	Watts.	27
Keep us, Lord, O keep us ever		81
Kingdoms and thrones to God belong	Watts.	26
Lamb of God, whose dying love	Wesley.	94
Lead, kindly light	Newman.	108
Let all the earth their voices raise	Watts.	23
Let us awake our joys	Kingsbury.	98
Let us with a gladsome mind	Milton.	65
Light of life, seraphic fire	Wesley.	71
Light of light, enlighten me	Schmolk, Winkworth.	70
Light of the lonely pilgrim's heart	Denny.	30
Like Israel's host, to exile driven	Ware.	25
Lo! He comes with clouds descending	Wesley.	84
Lo! He cometh, countless trumpets	Cennick.	84
Lo! on a narrow neck of land	Wesley.	49
Lo! what a glorious sight appears	Watts.	29
Long as I live I'll bless Thy name	Watts.	33
Look, ye saints, the sight is glorious	Kelly.	82
Lord, dismiss us with Thy blessing	Shirley.	85
Lord, from earthly cares set free		69
Lord, in the morning Thou shalt hear	Watts.	34
Lord Jesus, by Thy passion	Ikermann.	93
Lord of the vast creation	John Butmar.	95
Lord of the worlds above	Watts.	89
Lord, Thou hast been our	(Chant.)	114
Lord, Thou hast searched and seen me	Watts.	18
Lord, we come before Thee now	Hammond.	72
Lord, when we bend before	J. D. Carlyle.	45
Lord, with glowing heart I'd praise Thee	Key.	75
Loud hallelujahs to the Lord	Watts.	7
Love divine, all love excelling	Wesley.	78
Majestic sweetness sits enthroned	S. Stennett.	40
Many woes had Christ endured	Hart.	73
Morning breaks upon the tomb	Collyer.	65
Must Jesus bear the cross alone	G. N. Allen.	47
My country, 'tis of thee	S. F. Smith.	98
My days are gliding swiftly by	Nelson.	102
My dear Redeemer and my Lord	Watts.	19
My faith looks up to Thee	Ray Palmer.	97
My God, how endless is Thy love	Watts.	17
My God, how wonderful Thou art	Faber.	35
My God, my Father, blissful name	Steele.	45
My God, my Father, while	Charlotte Elliott.	101
My God, my King, Thy various praise	Watts.	9
My God, permit my tongue	Watts.	57
My God, the spring of all my joys	Watts.	38
My God, Thy boundless love I praise	H. More.	50
My never-ceasing song shall show	Watts.	33
My Saviour, my almighty Friend	Watts.	34
My soul, be on thy guard	Heath.	51

INDEX OF FIRST LINES. 137

First Line	Author	Page
Nearer, my God, to Thee	Sarah F. Adams.	97
No more, my God, I boast no more	Watts.	14
Not all the blood of beasts	Watts.	57
Now begin the heavenly theme	Langford.	63
Now be my heart inspired to sing	Watts.	10
Now be the gospel banner	Hastings.	90
Now from labor and from care	Hastings.	70
Now I resolve with all my heart	Steele.	12
Now to the Lord a noble song	Watts.	7
Now to the Lord who makes us know	Watts.	12
O be joyful in the Lord	(Chant.)	110
O bless the Lord, my soul	Montgomery.	53
O bread to pilgrims given	O esca, Palmer.	93
O come, let us sing	(Chant.)	111
O come, loud anthems	Tate and Brady.	7
O could I speak the matchless worth	Medley.	50
O could our thoughts and wishes fly	Steele.	44
O day of rest and gladness	Wordsworth.	90
O'er the distant mountains breaking	Monsell.	84
O'er the gloomy hills	W. Williams.	82
O for a closer walk with God	Cowper.	41
O for a heart to praise my God	Wesley.	44
O for a thousand tongues to sing	Wesley.	32
O great is Jehovah	Montgomery.	100
O happy day that stays my choice	Doddridge.	12
O help us, Lord, each hour of need	Milman.	21
O how I love Thy holy law	Watts.	44
O Jesus, King, most	Bernard, Caswall.	35
O Jesus, Thou the beauty art	Bernard, Caswall.	36
O Love divine, how sweet thou art	Wesley.	50
O mother, dear Jerusalem	Urbs beata.	37
O my soul, what means this sadness!	Fawcett.	85
One sweetly solemn thought	Phœbe Cary.	102
One sweetly solemn thought	(Adaptation.)	117
One there is above all others	Newton.	80
On Jordan's stormy banks	J. Stennett.	38
On the mountain-top appearing	Kelly.	83
O Paradise, O Paradise	Faber.	104
O render thanks to God above	Tate and Brady.	10
O sacred Head	Bernard, Gerhard, Alexander.	93
O Saviour, who for man	Coffin, Chandler.	11
O sing unto the Lord a new song	(Chant.)	111
O sweetly breathe the lyres above	Ray Palmer.	16
O Thou who hear'st the prayer	Toplady.	49
O Thou whose tender mercy hears	Steele.	43
Our blest Redeemer, e'er He breathed	Auber.	81
Our God, our help in ages past	Watts.	35
Our Lord is risen from the dead	Wesley.	23
O what if we are Christ's	Baker.	56
O where shall rest be found	Montgomery.	59
O wondrous type!	Celestis formam, Neale.	15
O worship the King, all-glorious	Grant.	106
O Zion tune thy voice	Doddridge.	86
Plunged in a gulf of dark despair	Watts.	47
Praise, everlasting praise be paid	Watts.	5
Praise the Lord, His glories show	Lyte.	62
Praise the Lord, ye heavens adore Him	Mant.	76
Praise to God, immortal	Anna L. Barbauld.	66
Praise ye Jehovah's name	Goode.	96
Praise ye the Lord, praise God	(Chant.)	110
Praise ye the Lord, praise ye	(Chant.)	110
Prayer is the soul's sincere desire	Montgomery.	41
Raise your triumphant songs	Watts.	52
Rejoice, all ye believers	Laurenti, Borthwicke.	92
Rejoice, the Lord is King	Wesley.	86
Ride on, ride on in majesty	Milman.	8
Rise, glorious Conqueror, rise	Milman.	96
Rise, my soul, and stretch thy wings	Seagrave.	94
Rock of ages, cleft for me	Toplady.	68
Round the Lord in glory seated	Mant.	76
Safely through another week	Newton.	4
Salvation, O the joyful sound	Watts.	30
Saviour, breathe an evening blessing	Edmeston.	79
Saviour, when in dust to Thee	Grant.	73
Saviour, who Thy flock art feeding	Muhlenberg.	79
Saviour, visit Thy plantation	Newton.	85
See Israel's gentle Shepherd stand	Doddridge.	42
Servant of God, well done	Montgomery.	60
Shepherd, with Thy tenderest love		70
Shepherd of tender youth	Clemens Alexandrinus.	97
Shine on our land, Jehovah, shine	Watts.	32
Show pity, Lord, O Lord, forgive	Watts.	21
Sing of Jesus, sing forever	Kelly.	104
Sing to the Lord, ye distant lands	Watts.	29
Softly now the light of day	Doane.	72
Soldiers of Christ, arise	Wesley.	51
Sometimes a light surprises	Newton.	95
Songs of praise the angels sang	Montgomery.	62
Son of God, to Thee I cry	Mant.	73
Stand fast in the faith	Brown.	105
Stand up and bless the Lord	Montgomery.	51
Stand up, my soul, shake off thy fears	Watts.	6
Stand up, stand up for Jesus	Duffield.	90
Sun of my soul, Thou Saviour dear	Keble.	19
Sweet is the work, my God, my King	Watts.	13
Sweet is the work, O Lord	Lyte.	54
Sweet peace of conscience	Heginbotham.	17
Sweet Saviour, bless us e'er we go	Faber.	25
Sweet the moments, rich	Allen, Shirley.	79
Swell the anthem, raise the song	N. Strong.	62
Swell the anthem	(Adaptation.)	122
Take my soul, thy full salvation	Lyte.	75
That day of wrath, that dreadful	Walter Scott.	22
The day is past and gone	Wm. J. Blew.	59
The eternal gates lift up	C. F. Alexander.	31
Thee we adore, eternal Lord	Watts.	23
The God of Abraham, praise	Olivers.	74
The God of harvest, praise	Montgomery.	93
The heavens declare Thy glory, Lord	Watts.	9
The Lord descended from above	Sternhold.	27
The Lord, how wondrous are His ways	Watts.	18
The Lord is my strength and song	(Chant.)	112
The Lord is King, lift up thy voice	Conder.	6
The Lord is my shepherd	(Adaptation.) 126,	127
The Lord is my shepherd	(Chant.)	113
The Lord is my shepherd, no want	Montgomery.	107
The Lord is my strength and new song	Chant.	112
The Lord is my strength	(Adaptation.) 119, 120,	121
The Lord Jehovah lives	Hastings.	89
The Lord Jehovah reigns and royal	Watts.	61
The Lord Jehovah reigns ; His throne	Watts.	89
The Lord Jehovah reigns. Let all	Watts.	52
The Lord my pasture shall prepare	Addison.	24
The Lord my shepherd is	Watts.	58
The Lord of glory is my light	Watts.	31
The Lord our God is full of might	Kirke White.	27
The Lord 's my shepherd, I'll not want	Rous.	42
The Lord will come, the earth shall	Heber.	22
The morning purples all the sky	A. R. Thompson.	33
Then will I sprinkle clean water	(Chant.)	114
There is a fountain filled with blood	Cowper.	46
There is a land of pure delight	Watts.	37
There is an hour of peaceful rest	Tappan.	41
The Saviour kindly calls	Doddridge.	59
The Saviour, O what endless charms	Steele.	40
The spacious firmament	Addison.	9
The strain upraise	Godescalcus, Neale, (Chant.)	109
The voice of free grace	Thornby.	103
The whole creation groans and waits		28
Thine earthly Sabbaths, Lord	Doddridge.	13
This is the day the Lord hath made	Watts.	23
Thou art the way ; to Thee alone	Doane.	45
Thou lovely source of true delight	Steele.	39
Thou only sovereign of my heart	Steele.	17
Thou who art enthroned above	Sandys.	69
Through all the changing	Tate and Brady.	44
Through every age, eternal God	Watts.	18
Through sorrow's night and	Kirke White.	46
Thus far the Lord hath led me on	Watts.	14
Thy name, almighty Lord	Watts.	51
Thy will be done	(Chant.)	104
Time is winging us away	Burton.	94
'Tis finished—so the Saviour cried	Stennett.	22

INDEX OF PSALMS.

		PAGE
'Tis midnight; and on Olive's brow	*Tappan.*	22
To God, the only wise	*Watts.*	54
To Jesus, the crown of my hope	*Cowper.*	99
To Thee, my God, my Saviour	*Hawels.*	91
To the source of every blessing	*Bathurst.*	70
To Thy pastures fair and large	*Merrick.*	76
To us a Child of hope is born	*Montgomery.*	31
To your Creator God	*Steele.*	88
To Zion's hill I lift mine eyes	*Tate and Brady.*	35
Unveil thy bosom, faithful tomb	*Watts.*	22
Upward I lift mine eyes	*Watts.*	89
Vainly through night's weary hours	*Lyte.*	79
Watchman, tell us of the night	*Bowring.*	69
We are on our journey home	*Charles Beecher.*	104
We give immortal praise	*Watts.*	86
Welcome, delightful morn	*Hayward.*	87
Welcome, sacred day of rest	*William Brown.*	66
Welcome, sweet day of rest	*Watts.*	53
Welcome, welcome, dear Redeemer		83
We lift our hearts to Thee	*J. Wesley.*	54
We praise Thee, O God	*(Chant.)*	115
What are these in bright array!	*Montgomery.*	66
What shall I render to my God!	*Watts.*	34
What sinners value I resign	*Watts.*	11
When all Thy mercies, O my God	*Addison.*	48

		PAGE
When gathering clouds around I view	*Grant.*	24
When I can read my title clear	*Watts.*	37
When I survey the wondrous cross	*Watts.*	19
When Jordan hushed his waters	*Campbell.*	11
When, Lord, to this our western land		49
When marshalled on the nightly	*Kirke White.*	11
When on Sinai's top I see	*Montgomery.*	71
When overwhelmed with grief	*Watts.*	58
When shall the voice of singing		90
When sins and fears prevailing rise	*Steele.*	12
When streaming from the eastern	*Shrubsole.*	25
When Thou, my righteous Judge	*Huntingdon.*	49
While shepherds watched	*Tate and Brady.*	38
While Thee I seek	*Helen M. Williams.*	48
While with ceaseless course the sun	*Newton.*	74
Why do we mourn departing friends	*Watts.*	47
Why should our tears		47
With all my powers of heart and tongue	*Watts.*	6
With glory clad	*Tate and Brady.*	5
With joy we hail the sacred day	*Lyte.*	31
With joy we meditate the grace	*Watts.*	40
Ye angels who stand round	*De Fleury.*	99
Ye nations round the earth, rejoice	*Watts.*	4
Ye servants of God, your Master	*Wesley.*	106
Yes, the Redeemer rose	*Doddridge.*	88
Yes, we trust the day is breaking	*Kelly.*	83
Your harps, ye trembling saints	*Toplady.*	60

INDEX OF PSALMS.

PSALM	HYMN
V.	147
XVII.	36
XVIII.	113, 392
XIX.	26, 28, 237
XXIII.	96, 182, 258, 315, 450, 467
XXIV.	95
XXVII.	132
XXXIV.	192
XLII.	168
XLV.	23, 30, 119
XLVI.	70, 469
XLVII.	118
XLVIII.	228, 239, 429
LI.	84
LV.	255
LVII.	5
LXI.	256
LXIII.	65, 210, 252
LXVII.	137, 302, 465
LXVIII.	108
LXIX.	88
LXXI.	145
LXXII.	22, 34, 403
LXXIII.	150
LXXXIV.	31, 46, 391
LXXXVII.	107, 330
LXXXIX.	116, 135
XC.	149, 408

PSALM	HYMN
XCI.	357, 358
XCII.	44
XCIII.	6, 10, 270, 390
XCV.	17, 227, 461
XCVI.	96, 123
XCVII.	7, 11, 12
XCVIII.	122, 461
XCIX.	230
C.	1, 3, 4, 430, 459
CIII.	32, 161, 235, 462
CIV.	447
CVI.	33
CVII.	20
CXVI.	148
CXVII.	21, 225
CXVIII.	120, 256
CXIX.	193
CXXI.	153, 389, 466
CXXII.	146, 269
CXXVII.	350
CXXXII.	139
CXXXVI.	14, 290
CXXXVII.	249
CXXXVIII.	15
CXLV.	27, 142
CXLVI.	94
CXLVIII.	18, 273, 334, 457
CL.	274, 417, 458

www.ingramcontent.com/pod-product-compliance
Lightning Source LLC
Chambersburg PA
CBHW020757230426
43666CB00007B/740